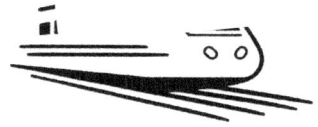

I HOPE THERE'S A KETTLE IN MY ROOM

PAULA ROONEY

Copyright

Second edition published 2025
First edition published 2022 Fortis Publishing

Copyright under exclusive license from Paula Rooney.
The rights of Paula Rooney have been asserted in accordance with the Copyright, Design and Patents Act 1998.
No part of this publication may be reprinted or reproduced or utilised or stored in any form or by any electronic, mechanical, or other means, now known or hereafter invented, without permission in writing from Paula Rooney.

ISBN: 978-1-0682765-0-7

This is a travel journal and the book was written in its raw form whilst the author travelled around Europe in the summer of 2020. Therefore, this is a true account of the author's trip.

Acknowledgements

It wasn't my intention to write a book, simply to record a trip of a lifetime for my own reference.

So, I would like to thank my friend, Tami Mundy, for being the first person I hesitantly asked to read my first completed draft. She immediately said she loved it and emailed me a sentence after she read every chapter. Without her encouraging words, it might have stayed a personal journal.

I then let my daughter, Ciara, read it, and then my mum. Much harsher critics than Tami. They both enjoyed it too, so I decided to approach a publisher.

Here, I need to thank Jessica Harrington for her kindness and for putting me in touch with Ken Scott. Thank you to Emily Ould from Emily Charlotte Editorial Services for helping to re-edit this second version of the book.

I want to thank everyone at Fortis Publishing for their warmth and professionalism during the creating of the first edition of this book. Ken Scott, for his videocalls and his help and advice, and Joan Elliott for her emails and encouragement, especially over a section I nearly deleted. Thank you to Dan Taylor for the cover design, which in this second edition, I have adapted. Thanks to Reinette Visser for her support in finalising the book.

About the Author

Paula Rooney was born in 1965 in Harlow, Essex, then spent several years in Ipswich, Suffolk, before settling in St Austell, Cornwall, in 2001 to raise her family.

Journaling holidays started with the first family holiday to Cornwall when she was 10, followed by a trip to Scotland and another trip to Cornwall. When she was 13, her dad left the family for good, taking the car with him.

Then, when Paula was aged 16, her mum took them on a holiday to a caravan park at Burnham-on-Sea. Paula, her sister, her brother, and her brother's friend, all went by bus, as Paula's mother didn't drive. It was a big adventure and lots of fun.

This might have ignited her passion for travel and instilled a sense of adventure. If you don't have a car, you get a bus. If you don't know where you are, look at a map.

Please follow all the social media accounts to keep up to date with the latest book releases and see where Paula is travelling at the moment.

You can find her as @PaulaRooneyAuthor on Facebook, Instagram, and TikTok.

Please visit www.paularooneyauthor.co.uk to find photos in the gallery section of the website to match this book. They even have page numbers so you know exactly where they were taken.

Dedication

To my children. You have all turned into amazing adults, living out your dreams. I am proud of you all.

To my mum, for passing on her survival skills I didn't know I had until I needed them.

To Phil, for his endless support.

Contents

1. Planning a Trip — 1
2. The Lockdown — 4
3. Truro to Paris — 9
4. Paris to Morzine — 18
5. Morzine — 25
6. Morzine to Montreux — 30
7. The Panoramic-Express — 36
8. Lake Como to Venice — 48
9. Venice — 57
10. Venice to Ljubljana — 65
11. Ljubljana — 72
12. Leaving Ljubljana — 89
13. Lake Bled — 100
14. Bled to Zagreb — 107
15. Zagreb — 118

16.	Croatia to Hungary	125
17.	Gyenesdiás	135
18.	Gyenesdiás to Znojmo	143
19.	Znojmo to Český Krumlov	151
20.	Český Krumlov	159
21.	Český Krumlov to Karlovy Vary	172
22.	Karlovy Vary	180
23.	Karlovy Vary to Mainz	186
24.	Mainz	192
25.	Mainz to Koblenz	197
26.	Koblenz	203
27.	Koblenz to Bacharach	209
28.	Bacharach	218
29.	Bacharach to Cologne	222
30.	Cologne	230
31.	Cologne to Cornwall	234
32.	Cornwall	242
33.	More info, some tips and tricks	246
34.	What I Spent	252
35.	Thank you, reader	253

Planning a Trip
Spring 2020

Life has essentially stopped in this village on the outskirts of Truro, Cornwall, in the spring of 2020. This new stillness and time out of life is unique. I have been yearning for some time like this for a long time. Time to just stop. Time away from parenting, working, budgeting, planning, and stressing. A window of time when I can do all the activities that I don't have time for.

One day, when I have time, I will ... well, here it is.

But while I have always hoped to find some time to myself one day, maybe a month off work, unpaid or something, I never would have imagined the whole world stopping as well. A pandemic. It's almost unimaginable and yet, here we are, living it.

The lockdown has given me lots of time to think, which has given me some clarity. I have decided that going on an adventure is absolutely what I want to do.

So, this is a true story/tale/adventure/diary of a very average, short (five-foot nothing), grey-haired and wrinkly, 55-year-old woman.

I didn't say 'normal'. I have never considered myself normal and none of us are average. There is no such thing. What I mean is, I am not famous. I haven't invented anything, no one has heard of me, well, not in big circles, so very similar to most of us. However, you can't have reached 55 without a few tales to tell.

Some of them I might even share with you on this journey.

In January this year, I moved in with my partner/boyfriend/other half/best friend – that's one person, not four – and his 17-year-old daughter, Maria. Phil has another daughter, Becky, who lives in Bristol with her boyfriend. My own four children, Liam, Aidan, Ciara, and Jamie, are all living independently now.

That is such a tiny sentence for something so big. After 25 years of intense parenting and a difficult divorce, it's a huge milestone in my life. All the kids are standing on their own two feet. I have given up the rented house and so my finances are back in order as well. The year 2020 has already been very important and I want to mark it in some way.

When you think about it, 55 is very old and yet, very young, depending on how you look at it. Am I too old to go on an adventure?

I do know that any dreams and plans have to be realistic, taking into account my dodgy knees. Walking the Great Wall of China, a previous dream, is probably not going to happen.

I have always wanted to go backpacking in Greece, but it was always a mere thought, just too far away to grab, not clear enough to put into a plan. To be fair, in the mid-80s, when I should have gone, I didn't know a single person who had actually done it. The internet wasn't around yet, there weren't any blogs or YouTube videos, no instant access to the world like we have today. So, it just didn't happen. If we had had the internet when I was 20, who knows, I think I would have been exposed to the delights of travel and definitely gone on a trip.

On Tuesday 14th April, Phil and I went on another walk around the quiet, car-free country lanes. Across fields full of spring flowers, bluebells, pink campion, white flowers of wild garlic, and trees full of pink blossom. We chat as always, easily exchanging views. Phil is happy for me to plan a trip, and he says he might do the same when the time feels right.

Back home, I immerse myself in travel YouTube videos. There are so many. Mostly by 18-year-olds, but that's OK, there's lots of useful advice on them about what to pack, what not to pack, which bag to take. I need to decide where to go, what month, and what to take with me. I need to decide whether to plan my trip in detail and book trains and accommodation, or just go. The videos are a great help with thinking through those decisions.

After much thought, I decide I will go for three weeks. To Eastern Europe. It looks lovely in all the videos and I think I will plan the first couple of days and then wing it. This will give me the freedom to change my mind if I want to stay somewhere for longer or leave earlier. The flexible approach appeals to me more, rather than booking every single destination and accommodation. To feel free on this trip is very important, having raised children for the last 25 years and having all those parental restraints. I want to feel free enough to make decisions based on what's happening on the trip. Wake up and change direction if I want to or stay somewhere longer. At the moment, I have no idea where I am going and that's very exciting.

The Lockdown
Monday 20th April

Boris says we have at least another three weeks of lockdown. I am still loving it, still enjoying the endless days of reading, chilling, gardening, walking, cooking, and researching my trip.

I have ordered a Post Office travel card, which seems one of the best ways to get money out abroad. I have also ordered an online bank account with an app, which apparently gives you a good exchange rate. I need to get savvy with all this.

I have been researching where to go in Europe. It's pretty huge, even if you have narrowed it down. How do you know where in Hungary to go? Which town? How to get there, how to get from there to Slovenia? Where to stay in Slovenia? For how long? It all seems very surreal just thinking about it. But also, very exciting.

So, I google, 'Nice places to go in Eastern Europe,' which is exactly what I want, and it gives lots of options. I am making notes of the ones that stand out and appeal to me the most. After researching each place that I like the look of, I have a vague plan. It's a start.

Prague, Bratislava, Budapest, Ljubljana, Mostar, Montenegro, and Croatia. A month ago, I didn't even know some of these places existed, let alone where they were on a map.

I make a conscious decision early on to avoid big cities like Munich, Brussels, and Paris. I prefer natural places, the countryside, spectacular views. Places you would get your camera out a lot. This is a little more challenging as I don't understand the rail system, but I am a quick learner. It says so on my CV.

Then I change my mind. I want to spend some time in Prague with Phil, and it's easy to get a flight there for a weekend. So, I find Český Krumlov , which is near Prague and looks lovely. I look in detail at Bratislava and what to do there and it doesn't appeal to me, so I replace it with Banská Bystrica. I think Budapest looks a bit dull, although I am sure it's not, and find Tapolca. Ljubljana is a must. My kids liked it there and it's a no-brainer of a place to go according to the Interrailing community on Facebook, so I must add it to my list.

The Interrail planner is good. It lets you put destinations onto a map so that you can plan your journey and see if there is a train station there. This is a whole new learning curve, but I am loving the planning side of it. I can't wait to actually go.

Monday 15th June

The shops have re-opened in England. Apparently, people were queuing in Birmingham overnight to get into Primark. I was hoping this lockdown will have altered people's perception of the world, changed us all slightly, for the better. I can't think of anything that is so important that you would want to queue all night for it. I am reading *The Survival of Jan Little* by John Man, a surprise gift from Phil. It's about a family living in the rainforest and how Jan survived the awful conditions and circumstances. They had almost nothing, as they were living so remotely, and ate half a tin of peaches between three of them for a wedding anniversary celebration. A huge contrast to the desperate need to buy a new pair of knickers in Primark.

Back in Cornwall, the roads are busy again, and now there is news of borders opening across Europe. Ciara, my daughter, is still waiting to hear about her job in Greece as a synchronised swimming entertainer, or the 'mermaid job' as we both have nicknamed it. And Liam, my son, will go straight into his summer season in Morzine, France, without his trip back to England to catch up with friends and get his summer clothes out of storage.

I am now hoping to travel for three weeks in September and October. If it's safe to do so. The route has changed again. All this time to research is good. The route currently is Roscoff to Venice, via Paris on the overnight train. Then after two days in Venice, over to Ljubljana, and then somewhere in Croatia to see the Plitvice Lakes, on to Mostar, and then Montenegro. I am not sure how long that's all going to take and whether I will fly home or meander back across Europe. But it's a plan. With the shops reopening, I am keen to buy a backpack and some items on my list.

Tuesday 21st July

I just booked my Interrail ticket! Hooray!

It starts on Sunday 2nd August. I have a confirmation email, so I didn't dream it. Sometimes I need to see things in black and white.

It was sort of impulsive and sort of not. I returned to work at the garden centre café on the 4th July after my lovely three months' furlough came to an end and thought I would go in September. I was going to ask for time off work, and keep a close eye on what was happening with the coronavirus in Europe. But work was miserable, so I handed in my notice. I have another part time job at the café at Wheal Martyn china clay museum near St Austell. I am not needed back yet as it's not busy enough. During the lockdown, I rediscovered my love for sewing, dusted off my sewing machine and opened an Etsy shop. I can't get stuck into that until I return, so I decide there is nothing stopping me from going now. It feels like the right time to do my first solo trip across Europe, and I am beyond excited.

I am closely watching the Re-open EU website and the Facebook Interrailing site. There are lots of people travelling now.

So, Dora is off to town to buy a backpack. This is Ciara's nickname for me, as I often have a small backpack on. I love bags of all types, but wearing a backpack is practical as you have your hands free, which was useful as a mum and a childminder, being able to hold the little ones' hands.

Wednesday 22nd July

This morning, I am thinking about important stuff. Money. How much do I need to leave in my bank? How much shall I put on my new banking app, how much on my Post Office card? I need to photocopy all my documents and print off the insurance.

I also just activated a new sim card on an old phone. I am taking two phones. Ciara and Liam had their phones stolen when they were backpacking in Europe and Aidan had his stolen in Paris at a Download festival.

I hope not to get mine stolen as it's going to be in my bag most of the time and I will only get it out when I absolutely need to. But, as a safety net, I am taking my old one, as I don't have the skills to buy and sort out phones and a new sim card in a foreign country. I would struggle in this country. Two phones will also be helpful as I will have two lots of data and hopefully one will always be charged. I will need to access the internet to book accommodation and trains. It really is vital that I have a functioning phone at all times.

I have changed my route again. To be honest, I don't mind where I go. I had picked out some stunning places but with the coronavirus, some countries are difficult to enter and I need to respect that and be grateful that I am travelling at all.

So I decide to go and see Liam in Morzine. I haven't seen him since I visited him in Brighton last October. And I would love to see where he is living. It looks so amazing in the photos that I have seen, and not somewhere that I would normally choose to go as I don't ski or snowboard. Just the thought of me on a pair of skis is ridiculous. Also, I can't take a ferry from Plymouth as they are not allowing foot passengers on at the moment.

I will get a train from Truro to Paddington, then over to St Pancras for the Eurostar to Paris and find somewhere to sleep. Plan the next leg to Morzine, then travel east, across Europe, maybe take the Panoramic-Express across Switzerland and maybe go to Venice. Who knows? I am so excited.

Truro to Paris
Sunday 2nd August

It's 8.47 am and I am on the train at Truro train station having watched Phil walk away, back to his car. That was difficult. I am super excited to be going on an adventure and he is going back to his normal life of working, cooking, cleaning, and parenting, which seems very unfair. Plus, I am going to really miss him.

I am sitting in my seat with my big backpack, small backpack, money belt, and a carrier bag of food. I am on my way to Paddington station and the train left one minute early.

I am literally shaking with nerves and excitement. My bag is the biggest that I have ever taken anywhere as I usually have a suitcase for this amount of stuff. I thought I had packed lightly with only minimal clothes, including only four pairs of knickers, but it's still a big bag.

I am not happy with the mask-wearing, but I just have to get used to it. With shaky hands, I have written the time of the train onto my Interrail pass. I don't want to be fined, so I had filled out the section of Truro to Paddington already, but I hadn't put the time in, in case it changed. I am not at all familiar with the form, or what I am supposed to do and I am really nervous that I might mess it up. It's my first entry on this blank Interrail sheet and I can't help but wonder what other destinations will be on it when I have completed my trip. I don't think I have ever felt so free and excited in my life.

I put it back in my money belt with my passport, which is under my top where no one can see it.

This all feels surreal. I am actually on the train but I still can't believe it. Little old me is going backpacking. I have stepped out of my life. The kids are all OK, Phil is OK and I am free to go exploring. After my life being so full of responsibilities for so long, this feels scary and amazing.

The last week has been strange. By last Saturday, I was 95% packed as I am not working anymore and I had a whole week to fill. Time seemed to slow down and speed up intermittently. On Tuesday, I cooked seven Bakewell tarts and a big batch of vegan spaghetti bolognaise, so that felt like a normal day. Well, that's a normal day for me, possibly not for others. Wednesday and Thursday I watched hour by hour slip by, wanting today to arrive but wanting to enjoy my time with Phil and spend time in the garden. I felt like I was on the edge of something life-changing, or at least an amazing, long trip around Europe to places that I don't know.

On Wednesday, I read *Educated* by Tara Westover. I started Tuesday evening and finished Wednesday evening. I thoroughly enjoyed it, obviously. Wednesday flipped over into Thursday. I went into town and then popped to Joanne's for a quick cuppa.

Friday was busy, with a trip to St Austell. I started with a mammogram, then picked my mum up, and we went to see my son, Aidan, at Hangloose, where he works. We met him in his lunch break to give him a present as it was his 25th birthday. A quick trip to the recycling centre, which took 45 minutes because of the new pandemic policies, then a long overdue haircut at my friend Tania's. After that, a quick visit to my friend, Tami's, and then I went to see my son, Jamie, for the first time since we left the rented house in January. It was nice to catch up and see him looking happy and settled.

Now I need to work out how to get to the loo. I had too much tea before I left the house and I really need to go. I decide to wait until we leave a station. I will then run to the loo, taking my small bag and leaving the big one. The floor of the toilet is wet, so I can't put my bag down. This is a challenge but I feel better, more comfortable, as they say. Success, my big bag is still there when I get back. It really wasn't going anywhere as the train didn't even stop, but I am a worrier. I hated leaving it as it has everything in it that I need for my trip. I am hoping my nerves and worrying don't get in the way.

I have free Wi-Fi on the train, so I start snoozing my Facebook groups: sewing, gardening, sourdough and Cornish weather. I don't need any of that. I have also found a socket so I can keep my phone charged. I message a few of my friends on Facebook. I haven't wanted to say anything to people as, to be honest, it felt like a dream. But now I am on the train, so it's really happening. They are all surprised to hear that I am on a train to Europe. It is quite a random thing to do, especially in a pandemic.

Now I'm going to try hard to chill and let Stephen Fry entertain me with his book. I can still feel the adrenalin going round but I will calm down soon.

It's 10.00 am and we have just arrived in Plymouth and had five carriages bumped and clicked into place. I am feeling a little peckish. All the nerves have used up my reserves of melon, pineapple, and my delicious homemade granola. So, as a treat I made some focaccia bread yesterday with oodles of rosemary from the garden. I am going to have that now, as I think my tummy has settled down enough. But then I will need a drink and then I will need a wee. It's an endless cycle, and the train is filling up now.

I have never seen such an array of face masks. Everyone except one man is wearing one. I wonder if you can take it off to eat focaccia. If that's the case, I might nibble a bit all the way to

London, although it's very stuffy and annoying. No, I have to respect the mask-wearing and be grateful I am travelling, but I will eat some bread.

It's delicious, just enough salt on top and a thin layer of spread. Oh dear, it's given me hiccups, that's not good on a busy train. I don't know why bread does that to me.

I fumble in my bag for the new granny chain that I bought on Etsy for my glasses. Losing my glasses is something I do hourly at home. I only need them for distance so they are on and off my head, and already I have been searching for them on the seat next to me. So, they are going on my new funky chain, trying to look modern, and failing miserably.

By Totnes, I feel calm again, so calm that I can't believe that I am going to Europe on my own. I need to drink some of this litre of orange juice that I brought with me or my third bag, a carrier full of food, is going to be heavy on the London underground.

At Taunton, I treat myself to the salad that I brought with me. I get to christen my new spork, or whatever it's called, the all-in-one spoon fork and knife, and have some more focaccia. I hope Phil and Maria are enjoying the other half as much as I am. It's utterly divine.

I hope Phil is OK. He was OK about me going, and he understands why I want to go. But he is obviously worried about me too. I have told him I will message him as often as I can. Same with my mum, just send random texts saying where I am, without the need for a reply.

The train is about an hour and a half from Paddington. Ooh! It's gone very well so far.

When I get off the train at Paddington station, the ticket lady wants to see my train ticket. That's a big ask. I am wearing the big backpack, which has clips to hold the smaller one onto your front, which is very clever. But it means I can't get to my money belt, which is under my clothes, under the bag hanging off my front. So, I have to step to one side and fumble for the zips in my money belt underneath everything. I can't see anything. It's a bit like being heavily pregnant. I sort it out, but I have an extra food bag which is a step too far. I go through the barrier, but then realise that I have the contents of my money belt hanging out, so I stop and sort myself out. It's all a bit overwhelming and I feel quite uncomfortable with all these bags hanging off me. I also feel very responsible for myself. I know how to navigate a train station, but today I have so many bags. I am excited but also very flustered.

I get my debit card out, ready to buy an underground ticket, which I am not sure how to do. When I worked in London at Fortnum and Mason's, aged 18, I had a yearly ticket that I just showed or used at the barrier. I have been to London since then, but the technology seems to change with every visit.

Anyway, the lady explains that I just zap my card rather than buy a ticket and they charge me later when I get off. A good idea, I think. I get off after one stop at Edgeware Road, and while I am waiting for the train, I look for my card to make sure it's safe. I can't find it.

I've only been one stop on the Underground and I've lost my credit card already. I am standing at a bench on the platform, and I look everywhere, getting in a fluster. I am heavy with bags and it feels cumbersome. I unclip my front bag and look inside, and there it is. I had put a karabiner on the bag for security and it only opens a small way, and I don't remember putting anything in there. I feel a bit unsure and scared. I am familiar with the London Underground, and I have walked around with my money belt undone and temporarily lost my card. Perhaps this is going to be a disaster. I haven't even left England yet.

I tell myself that it's early days, and I am not familiar with these new bags. There are lots of pockets and I don't know where everything is going to live. It does make me wonder how

I am going to cope in Europe if I can't cope in London. I feel a little unsure of myself. I do hope this trip was a good idea.

So, here I am at St Pancras International Railway station to get the Eurostar to France. I go through passport control which is very strange at a train station. I am given a bright yellow boarding pass for the Eurostar, my destination, Gare du Nord. That's so French. Then I get a very much-needed takeaway tea and plonk myself down on a seat.

I message Phil to give him an update and he says it's not sunk in yet that I won't be home for tea. I feel a little selfish, but it's my time to go on this adventure. He still has parenting duties, so we couldn't have gone together. And I wanted to go solo on this trip to see if I can navigate myself around Europe. To find out what I am made of and have some freedom and fun.

It's unusual here at St Pancras station. It feels like an airport, but instead of being white and bright like an airport with big windows, it's dark like a train station. Yet, it has the feel of an airport with all the chairs and people waiting to be called. The whole process is a combination of train and plane.

At 3.25 pm, I am on the Eurostar, it should leave at 3.31 pm. Because of COVID-19, no one is sitting next to me, which suits me. I can now relax and enjoy the journey.

I am quite excited about going under the Channel and experiencing something new.

I worked for a market research company when I was about 23. It was one of the strangest jobs that I have ever done, knocking on doors trying to interview people about biscuits or shampoo. I once interviewed a lady in her knickers and bra as she ironed her dress for work. It was kind of her to let me in. Maybe I begged her, it's possible, as it was a difficult job. One job was to ask people on their doorsteps why they chose a particular airline for their holiday, and a couple invited me in. That was kind of them, as it's a lot easier to fill out the forms sitting down, but they got all their photo albums out from their holidays and I couldn't escape. Then there was the man with a strange look in his eye who invited me in. I definitely refused, as he was very odd.

But one job was all about the building of the Eurotunnel, and what facilities people wanted at the terminals. It was such an incredible idea back then to build the tunnel. So, it's interesting to see what the results are. I don't see a play area which I'm sure was quite high up the list. I also did the same Eurotunnel survey on a ferry from Felixstowe to Zeebrugge. I went back and forth twice in 48 hours without getting off, and I loved it. I had a captive audience who had free time, were interested in the questions, and didn't slam their doors in my face and I hung out in the staff room. It was fun.

This looks and feels like a train, but it sways left and right slightly, making me feel a little sick, or maybe it's too much orange juice and focaccia. And my ears keep popping. It's odd to think we are under the sea. It's black through the glass, like we are in a very long tunnel, which we are, and there are no stops or stations to whizz by. So, it's just a long journey with no stops, in the dark, swaying a bit. I have no idea how fast we are going as there's no scenery to compare it to.

An hour later, we pop up in France, with flat fields and blue sky, easy as that.

The train arrives at Gare du Nord train station in Paris. I go out of the station doors and I am greeted by busy, noisy Paris. People everywhere, and cars and buses on the busy roads.

I make my first mistake.

Where is the hotel? I forgot to draw a map. My first rule was not to stand around on street corners with my phone out looking up at street signs.

Fail. That's exactly what I did.

Fortunately, I had already looked at the map when I booked the hostel and somehow I remember which direction to go in, and after briefly checking my phone on a street corner, I go the right way. I walk confidently, as Phil suggested, trying not to look lost, and get to the hostel as quickly as I can. Luckily, it's not far. Well, not luckily, that's why I booked it.

At 8.06 pm, I am in the hostel bar, eating chips and drinking cider. I feel like a backpacker, which makes me smile. I am in my very first hostel, apart from the one in Wales on a geography school trip when I was doing my O-Levels. That was haunted, and me and my friend, Sue, heard a ghost screaming out, 'Fire!' which was very frightening. This hostel is modern and nowhere near as old as that remote Welsh stone-built one, so I don't think anything like that will happen here.

The hostel, St Christopher's hostel, Gare du Nord, has a young vibe, music blaring, just as I expected. Because of COVID-19, the ten-bedroom dormitory will only have five women, so that's a bonus.

I look around the bar and I just simply can't believe I am in a hostel in Paris. I was in Cornwall this morning and I haven't been on a plane either. There's a lot for my brain to take in. The bar has tall glass ceilings and whilst I might be one of the oldest people here, I don't feel out of place. I love it.

I go outside to ring Phil, and the noise of the traffic is deafening. A man walks by with a stereo system on his shoulder, like he is out of *Fame*, the old television show that I loved back in the eighties.

I am very tired. I have been sitting down for most of the day but tired all the same. Pleased that I have managed to get from Truro to Paris very easily, as it's quite a long way.

I go up to my room, get ready for bed, and use the shared bathroom outside my room. The room is exactly as it looked in the photos, which is a relief. It's big and clean, with 10 bunk beds, and each has a red privacy curtain and a big lockable container under the bed. It's perfect. I hide behind my red curtain. It's very cosy, it has a little shelf to put my glasses and earrings on, it has a plug for my phone charger, and a little light. I must remember not to leave anything here.

I put a post on Facebook to tell everyone that I am in Paris on my own, on the first leg of my Interrail trip. I get such a lovely response from everyone. It's a surprise to most of them that I am going backpacking on my own. I am going to post every day, something small with a few photos so that I don't have to message people individually. It's a much more efficient way of letting everyone know that I am safe.

I have an early start tomorrow, so I go to sleep.

Paris to Morzine
Monday 3rd August

It's 8.10 am and I slept as well as I could, being in such a noisy spot, five minutes' walk from the Gare du Nord train station. The other women in my dorm all went to sleep early, and we never said a word to each other. So far, so good for making new friends and interacting with other backpackers.

I reach the train station by 7.08 am, which is incredibly early for me, but I have the length of France to travel today and then onto Morzine, which is not an easy place to get to. It doesn't have a train station and the buses are sketchy. I queue at the ticket office and the man tries to find me a train to Thonon-les-Bains for 7.45 am. I plan to then get a bus to Morzine.

Although I have an Interrail pass, I have to book a reservation on the high-speed trains and pay a fee. The 7.45 am is full, as they only let a certain number of Interrail people on. The ticket attendant tries to book me on the 10.23 am, which is now €20 instead of €10 as it's the last seat, but it turns out to be first-class only which my ticket doesn't cover me for.

Oh dear, this is not going well. I should have come straight back and sorted this out last night, but there were too many men hanging around on street corners looking dubious, so I didn't feel comfortable doing that.

I am feeling confident though, as the times of trains he is quoting me are the ones that I had been researching on the Interrail app. This means that I am getting the hang of the app and timetables. The next train to Thonon-les-Bains is €12-something, so I think fast as I don't want to hold up the queue.

If I get the later train, I might not get to Liam's this evening and I will have to pay for accommodation somewhere. So, I ask for a train to Geneva. It's the nearest big place, so I am thinking if I just get there, I will have done most of the travelling through France. From there, I will see what time it is and decide what to do next. This train I'm offered to Geneva turns out to be the 10.23 am, that I was just told there was no room on, so I am a little confused. The ticket attendant prints me a ticket anyway and it now costs €27.00. My ticket says I should be in Geneva at 1.29 pm. That's a super-fast train.

The only problem is, I am at the wrong train station. I thought I was at the right one, so this unnerves me a bit. Now I have absolutely no idea where to go. I am also hungry. There was no breakfast on offer at the hostel because of the COVID-19 situation and my stress levels are rising. I thought I was leaving from this station.

I queue up for a metro ticket. There are machines, but I couldn't figure out how to use them in London and I sort of know my way around London. So, it's best that I try to talk to a human, even if it's a French human. The ticket costs €1.90. I find a train which I think is the correct one to Gare de Lyon station and hesitantly get on it. It's a double-decker, how exciting. Well, I would be excited if I wasn't feeling like a lost hippopotamus. I feel awkward with my big backpack and obviously look like I am out of my comfort zone. People are bustling and jumping on the metro as I used to when I worked in London. They are all in a hurry to get to work. I have to decide whether to take steps down or up. I choose down and perch on the edge of a seat. I can't sit back because my backpack is taking up all of the chair.

Two stops later, and I am at Gare de Lyon. That was easy. It's like another airport terminal, but with low ceilings. I have found the 10.23 am to Geneva on the screen, so I sit down in a waiting area and take off my backpack. It's very heavy and cumbersome. I can't see any trains at all, just gates to go through. The trains must be on the other side, or upstairs or downstairs.

I assume that I wait for instructions as it doesn't leave for two hours. I didn't do this part of the journey very efficiently but there's nothing I can do about that now. I haven't missed anything, I just haven't been very efficient and put myself under a little bit of stress. So, I drink some more orange juice and eat the fruit pot that I brought for occasions like this and eat the last bit of now-stale focaccia and watch people coming and going. Two hours is a long wait and I could have stayed in bed longer if I had booked a train last night, but it's OK. I am on holiday.

The 10.23 am from Gare de Lyon to Geneva is on the platform and it looks very important. I have been through the barriers and worked out how to get on the train. It's a double-decker again but I don't venture upstairs with my backpack.

It's a very smooth ride, as you would expect on a high-speed train. I watch France whizz by outside the window. It turns from flat to mountainous the further south we travel. I go to the upstairs toilet so that I can look out of the window and experience being upstairs on a train. It's like being on a bus.

I message Liam about the bus to his house, and after lots of messages back and forth, with him making a few phone calls, he tells me the bus I planned on getting to his house only runs in the winter when the ski season is on. He organises a transfer bus from the airport directly to his house. He describes the house and gives me the key code as he will be at work. I am very grateful. The bus I planned on getting to Thonon-les-Bains would have been a disaster, so it's all worked out OK. I only have a couple of days with Liam, and then I will be totally on my own.

Any mistakes that I make when I move on from Morzine, I am going to have to sort out for myself.

Geneva is interesting, and I can't quite believe that I am here, in Switzerland. It's big and busy but feels clean. There are trams and bendy buses on the road and lots of people. I struggle around with my backpack on, looking for a café or cheap place to get a bowl of chips.

Eventually, after too much walking around in the drizzle, with my bag cutting into my shoulders, I find a patisserie. I have always wanted to go in one of these with all the little macaroons in the window, looking pretty. It's called Tea Room Martel. It isn't that posh inside, but that's probably best, as I bundle in with my huge damp backpack on. I have a posh tea and a tiny minuscule macaroon. My first ever macaroon, so why not my first in Switzerland? My bill is €6.00, which isn't so bad.

I have a wander down to the river and it's a bit drizzly. There is a huge road that takes a while to cross, but on the other side there isn't much to do except look at the fountain in the middle of the lake. But this is Lake Geneva and I am in Switzerland. I was in France earlier and England yesterday. I can't quite believe what's happening. It's very noisy and busy. Ciara came here and ran out of things to do in a day, and now I understand.

So, my trip to Geneva is short, but memorable. The women are all well dressed in expensive shoes and smell of posh perfume. They even have small fuzzy dogs that seem to match their outfits. The shops are Rolex and Hilfiger, not Poundland and TK Maxx. I am not sure I would want to spend any more time here, but I am also very happy to have visited Switzerland.

Time is short anyway. This is just a short stop enroute to Morzine. I head back to the train and bus station to work out how to get to the airport, where I am picking up the bus transfer.

It is all a bit complicated. I could get a train or a bus, but I can't work out how to do either. Then I spot two girl backpackers getting a ticket from a machine. They are friendly and offer to help me get a train ticket. I decide I have been on enough trains for one day and I want to get the bus so that I can get a better sense of where I am.

The buses are very frequent, every few minutes, unlike Cornwall, where you could wait hours, and often they don't turn up at all, or just drive by full. I have plenty of time and I watch a bus come and go. People get on in the middle doors and don't talk to the driver. So, you must need a ticket first. I notice the brand of the bus and then see a matching machine. Then I have to ask for help as I can't work it out. I get a €3.00 ticket but possibly paid too much as later I see that there is a €1.00 option. Anyway, it's done. I get on the next bus and no one even asks to look at my ticket. It is a nice ride around the town, there is a pharmacy on every corner. Geneva people are either very well or very ill.

I get to the airport and walk the entire length of shops and digital displays, only to find out that I am in the train station. It looks just like an airport terminal. I have to walk all the way back, my bag cutting into my shoulders. It's been on my back a lot today. My feet are still good, these are brilliant shoes. I did something right. My bag is good too, I have just been carrying it a lot today, and it's incredibly heavy.

As I walk back the length of the train station, I refresh my bad school French by trying to read all the moving digital adverts in an attempt to distract myself from the pain in my shoulders. The airport is literally through a door, which is very convenient and a shame that I missed it. I find out where I need to be and collapse into a chair.

It is 4.46 pm and the transfer Liam organised for me is at 6.00 pm.

I put my heavy bag down and open a lentil salad that I bought in the Co-op in Geneva. I hesitantly taste for chilli. I don't know what chilli is in Swiss or French, but I don't want my tongue to fall off. There is chilli in the lentils, but it's just bearable, which is good because my stomach is having spasms, it's so hungry. One tiny macaroon was never going to fill me up.

I am so looking forward to seeing Liam and chilling for a few days and giving him his few gifts to make my bag a little lighter.

It's been a long couple of days, with lots of miles covered from Cornwall to Geneva, but I think that's the biggest journey that I will do on the whole trip. I did enjoy it all, though and I can't wait to get to Morzine.

There are four of us on the transfer, a small minibus. The others are lads about Liam's age, all holding huge round bags, which I am guessing are bikes, but I have no idea.

The trip to Morzine is lovely. It gets more and more scenic the closer I get. Sweeping green hills with pretty chalets on them. There are some tricky roads, up high with big drops down, which I don't like much. Then, as you get nearer to Morzine, there are lots of posters and signposts with skiing photos on them. It's very exciting. I have never been anywhere like this.

Then we arrive in Morzine, and it's a picture postcard. Deep in a lush green valley with chalets climbing up the hills and every building, whether a shop or a café, is a wooden style chalet and so pretty. There is a river outside Liam's place with a little bridge and flowers everywhere. It's like another world and I am so grateful to be here. And if Liam hadn't got a job here, I probably would never have come because I don't do skiing or mountain biking.

Liam is at work, so I drop my bags off at his house, using the code for the key that he's already given me. I make myself a much-needed cup of tea, with oat milk, and grab a piece of cake that he has left out for me. He knows his mother well. I chill for a bit. Liam has left the radio on and I am listening to the French radio presenters, not understanding any of it.

Then, feeling a bit more refreshed, I leave the house and wander around a little, taking a few photos. It gradually turns dark and the roundabout near Liam's house has a church on it with lights and flowers. It is very pretty.

I see Liam walking down the hill from work and he looks so happy in his surroundings. He keeps in touch a lot and sends photos but to actually see him in the town where he lives and works is lovely. We head straight to an outside eating place, have a drink and some curly fries, followed by some cider and a good catch-up. I like it here.

Morzine
Tuesday 4th August

Today it's cloudy and Liam is disappointed. But I am certainly not, because I am in one of the most beautiful spots I have ever been in. Well, maybe that's not true as I live in Cornwall and there's nothing quite like walking on the vast Cornish cliffs.

Here, the beauty is different. The clouds are hanging low, spoiling the view that Liam is desperate to show me, but the clouds are adding to the atmosphere, making a roof over Morzine, turning it cosier and more unique.

I didn't know you could go on a ski lift if you weren't skiing. I don't know what I was expecting to do in Morzine, but it definitely didn't include ski lifts. My focus coming here was to see Liam and see where he is living, which is what parents like to do. Check in on your children, even if they are 26 years old. That would have been enough.

I knew from the photos he has shared with us that it is pretty here. Maybe I thought we would go for a walk, eat nice food, chat and catch up.

The ski lifts, I learn, are the key to this resort. It's so obvious now that I am here, but I had never given it any thought before. In winter, the mountains are covered in snow and used for snowboarding. In the summer, it's a mountain biking resort, using the same hills to ride down the grass. It's all making sense.

We queue up for the lift and it's a busy area. I am nervous. I get in a pickle, trying to zap my pass, and hold people up. Men with mountain bikes are far more efficient than me and keep their lift pass in their pockets so that it zaps as they pass through the gate. Me, I am fumbling about, not sure what to do.

There is so much mud, it's all over the floor, in the ski lift car, on the seats. The men are so caked in it you can't make out their clothes; they are just wearing mud. There is excitement, a buzz in the air. They are so keen to get back up to the top and ride back down.

We have to wait for a mud-free pod, which doesn't take long. They keep a couple free of mud and we go up the mountain.

We are at the top of Mont Chéry, as high as the clouds, at an altitude of 1,816 metres. I don't understand the numbers, but we are very high up.

Not far away, a paraglider jumps off the edge and hangs around in the air, weaving patterns in the sky, entertaining us.

The views are incredible, lush green mountains, and some capped with snow in the distance. It is stunning. It's all so big and I feel very small, even smaller than normal. This is nature at its best, unspoiled and vast. We can see the village of Morzine down below which, from here, looks so tiny. On the opposite side of the valley, you can see the straight vertical lines of the ski lifts cut out in the trees. It is cloudy, yes, but I think that adds to it.

We then walk across a mountain ridge which feels more like a wooded area. We walk through deep pine trees. It's really pretty and tranquil, and then we go down into Les Gets, the neighbouring village. We go to a café called Wild Beets Kitchen, where Liam brought Ciara on her visit. The food is perfect. I enjoy a really good, substantial salad with lentils, coleslaw, quinoa, and broccoli which is really yummy and nutritious, just what I need. Liam has a fat, toasted wrap that looks really good.

After lunch, we go on another lift to the top of the opposite mountain and look back across the valley at the ridge we were on earlier, before catching a lift back down to take the bus to Morzine. It's just a short journey but it saves our legs after all that walking.

Liam goes out with some friends in the evening, and I chill in the bath, which is a treat. I write a Facebook post, read my book, and go to sleep.

Wednesday 5th August

Liam has another great day planned and we are blessed with beautiful blue skies. We have breakfast in his house, of baked beans, mushrooms, and focaccia that we made yesterday. It's a great start to the day.

We go in a different direction, away from the town this time, and walk along a path towards another ski lift. On the way, Liam points to a huge, tall mountain in front of us called Nyon and says we are going to the top of that. He must be joking; it is huge, and dominating.

We take two sets of lifts to the top, stopping halfway. So, it's not as adventurous or as hard work as it sounds. The top is a bit sketchy for me. I have lost some confidence since breaking my ankle as I know how quickly and unexpectedly accidents can happen, but Liam is like a mountain goat.

There is a smallish area at the top. I thought mountains had points as you draw in a picture, but they are ragged, decent-sized pieces of land. Not quite as scary as you would think from the bottom, although I do watch my footing as it is a horribly long way down.

The views are truly breath-taking. Mountain after mountain as far as the eye can see. I just can't believe I am standing at the top with Liam. Morzine is tiny down below us, everywhere you look is a photo opportunity. The clouds have disappeared and I can now see why Liam was disappointed yesterday. Mont Blanc is just visible in the distance, with its snow-capped tip. We have some great photos taken of us which is lovely. The weather is perfect, with beautiful blue skies and green mountains. It's very special. Going to the top of a mountain was not something I ever thought I would do.

The journey down in an open chair lift is a little scary though. I am not good with heights – well, it's not the heights as such, but the dangling, and we are definitely dangling. There is a single piece of wire taking our open chair lift down to the bottom. If I were to drop something, it would drop hundreds of feet and never be seen again.

With the blue sky above, there is a stillness, a peacefulness, and a connection with nature. I am very scared but I try to relax and enjoy it for Liam's sake as he is showing me his town and all that it offers. I don't want him to know how scared I am. I will have to get out of my comfort zone on this trip to get the best out of it.

Everywhere you look is amazing. The lift is very steep, and I am scared, thrilled, and happy all at the same time. A man passes us going up and is looking at his phone, which surprises me, but Liam says you get used to it and it's a nice chill time. You don't always want to look at the view. I take in every bit as I am only here for a couple of days, not months or years.

In the afternoon, we go up another mountain. Again, the scenery is breath-taking. Liam points out the slope Ciara skied down, which obviously looks very different now with no snow, but it is lovely to think Ciara has enjoyed Morzine as well. Aidan and Jamie would enjoy it here too, having spent most of their teenage years at Poltair park, skating and scootering. Jamie went snowboarding in Bulgaria and Aidan would love it here too. I wish sometimes that I was rich and could pay for them all to join Liam out here.

We were going to walk to the lake, but the ground is very boggy after the recent rain and, after breaking my ankle once, I don't want to do it again. We try to walk, but we are slipping about in the squelch and it isn't easy. So, we go to the viewing platform for the lake instead. Liam has sent pictures of this lake, and I can't believe I am here looking down at it, so turquoise, nestled in the mountains. It reminds me of the water that you find around St Austell near the china clay pits and I'm a little disappointed that we can't get closer. Liam would have liked a swim, but we'd have to walk another two hours which won't be easy after the rain from the past few days.

So, we go for a coffee instead, well, cider for me as I am on holiday. The café is a wooden chalet, perched on the edge of the mountain at the halfway point to swap lifts. It is so picturesque, like something out of Hansel and Gretel. This is a lovely way to spend an hour, with such stunning scenery and a delicious cold cider.

Back at home, Liam cooks us dinner. A lovely stir-fry and rice which is delicious and very welcome after all that exercise. I have another bath and chill. Liam goes out again, which I am very happy about. I want him to see his friends as these are his days off from work, and we have been nattering all day.

I need to decide if I am leaving tomorrow or the day after. It's lovely here, but I want to start my solo trip, leave the security of Liam and wander around Europe on my adventure.

Morzine to Montreux
Thursday 6th August

It's 8.00 am and I am still not sure whether to leave today. It's lovely here, and spending time with Liam is precious, but I am itching to carry on with my journey. I want to continue the solo trip now and see where my adventure takes me.

I like my own company, which is why travelling alone doesn't bother me. Though I am concerned that I will get lost, or make the wrong decisions and lose things, I'm not afraid to be alone. Some people are introverts and some extroverts, and I am definitely an introvert. I want to do this adventure on my own to see what happens. There will be stories to tell, but I don't know what they are yet. I like the excitement of not knowing where I am going, where will I sleep next, a hostel a hotel? Can I navigate myself around Europe on my own?

I think I will leave today, so I go to the bus ticket office at 9.00 am to try and get a bus to Thonon-les-Bains. I manage to communicate with the lady in my basic school French. She even prints me a ticket, but I didn't do as well as I thought as she tells me I have to go from Thonon-les Bains back to Geneva to get to Montreux, which is my next destination. It seems that you can't get from Thonon-les-Bains to Montreux along the south of Lake Geneva for some reason. You have to leave from Geneva and go over the top of the lake.

I walk out, leaving the ticket on the counter. There's no point going from here to Thonon-les-Bains on a bus and getting a bus back to Geneva. It would take hours. It's probably cheaper but would take quite a while, and then I have to get to Montreux if I want to go on the Panoramic-Express.

I pick up a fresh baguette for breakfast from Liam's favourite bakery and then go back home. We decide it's best to get the transfer back to Geneva, then get the train to Montreux. So we, well Liam, gets that sorted for me and I get an email for a transfer at 11.30 am.

We squeeze in a quick trip to the waterfall. It's a lovely walk along a flat path that follows the stream from his house, then goes through a wooded area with tall, straight pine trees. The waterfall is bigger than I was expecting and Liam goes in for a swim. What a place to swim in the mornings. He says it is freezing but enjoyable. I don't take part. I dip my toe into the cold water and that's enough for me.

Then we enjoy a quick cup of coffee and tea, back in the middle of Morzine, on the outside seating. We are surrounded by wooden chalet-style shops just in case I haven't seen enough.

Soon, it's time to get my bus and say goodbye, not knowing when I will see him again.

It's been a lovely few days and my bag is a little lighter. I leave a pair of sunglasses with Liam, I hadn't realised that I had packed three, and I give him his gifts. He loves the new toiletry bag I have made him and compliments me on my sewing skills and choice of colours. He really does like it. I have thoroughly enjoyed seeing him thriving in Morzine and I am so lucky to have been somewhere so stunning.

So, I arrive back in Geneva where the minibus picked me up a few days ago, where I now get a train to Montreux. My head is full of lovely memories.

The train slides along the edge of Lake Geneva, which is a vast lake of bright blue water, framed by the mountains. Over the other side of the lake is a backdrop of very tall, dense mountains.

I take a closer look at my map and work out why I have been struggling with Thonon-les-Bains. There are no trains on the south side of Geneva because it's full of mountains.

Montreux is on the far right of Lake Geneva, but you have to travel on the left side and over the top of the lake. It all makes sense now. And, what a blessing I couldn't get a train from Paris to Thonon-les-Bains as I would have wasted time going back to Geneva.

This feels like the beginning of my trip now. I am in Switzerland and I don't have a bed booked for tonight, yet I am OK with that. I feel remarkably chilled. The view is stunning outside of the train window of the huge blue lake, the blue sky, and the mountains have white tips. It's a beautiful, scenic ride.

I arrive in Montreux. I don't have anywhere to sleep, as I only booked the minibus at 9.30 am this morning. I did look at a few options at Liam's house and there was a room in a hostel, so that's my plan. There will be hotels if nothing else, although everything looked very expensive.

I walk for half an hour from the train station to the hostel, which feels like an hour with my slightly lighter, but still very heavy yet bearable, backpack. I stop briefly at the tourist information as my phone and Wi-Fi won't work in Switzerland. The lady tells me there are vacancies at the hostel and gives me directions. I stay on the path that follows the lake, which is twinkling in the sunlight. It's a long walk but so nice, along a tree-lined, wide promenade. The planting is stunning. The trees frame the view of the water and mountains, and everything is clean and neat. Everything is blue now, the sea, the sky. Morzine was lush and green.

It's a sunny day and all along the lake people are enjoying the water. There are little jetties or steps down into the very inviting-looking water. Some people are swimming, some are on boats or paddleboards and it's so peaceful. What a place. Phil would love it here, as would all the children. They would get in the water and have fun.

Eventually I arrive at the Auberge de Jeunesse hostel. Thankfully, they have a bed in a women's dorm for me. It's €50 for a shared room in a hostel, wow. We are in Switzerland and nothing is going to be cheap here. I am only staying here so that I am in the best spot to get the Panoramic-Express tomorrow.

The lady at reception says I need one Swiss franc for the locker. I don't have one, so we swap a euro for a franc. Then, I remember I paid for my macaroon and tea in euros. I left them on the table, as the staff were all busy. I wouldn't say I slid out unnoticed, more like a cumbersome tortoise, but it seems I paid in the wrong currency. Oops.

The room is fine, nothing outstanding and not as modern as the Paris hostel. It has brown, old-fashioned bunk beds, but it's clean and comfortable looking. I am sharing it with a German girl and we have a brief conversation about where we have come from and where we are going. I have not made an everlasting friend, but it is nice to briefly chat with her. I dump my stuff and go off to explore. I walk for about two hours, back the way that I had walked from the train station and on a bit further, this time with more pleasure, without my rucksack.

Getting McDonald's chips and a BBQ dip for dinner is utterly disgraceful, but I am not paying the ridiculous prices for dinner. It's quite busy and I don't want to sit in a restaurant by myself. The hostel has breakfast, so I am looking forward to that in the morning.

I sit in the chill room on the ground floor of the hostel. There's only me in it and I lay out all my maps and notepad on a table. You can only get Wi-Fi downstairs and not in the rooms, so I am all set up to do some research. From the table, I have a view of the lake through an archway. That's probably one of the reasons that this hostel costs so much, because the location and the views are stunning. The sun sets while I write my journal and I pop out to take some great photos. Phil rings me, as I can't seem to get my phone to work in Switzerland and we have a chat.

I look at my map and try to work out what to do next. I am in Montreux to take the Panoramic-Express tomorrow, which I am super excited about. I know that they go every hour from the train station as I asked when I arrived. I am not making the same mistake that I made in Paris. From now on, I will ask any questions that I have at the station when I arrive and then I am prepared.

The Panoramic-Express ends at Lucerne and I haven't decided what to do after that. I don't know whether to stay there or move on. And I am not exactly sure what to do after that. I think it might be Venice, but I am not getting excited at the thought of Venice. I think it's going to be very touristy but I am so close that maybe I should visit and at least have a chance to like it or dislike it.

I can study my options once I get to Lucerne. I am not sure what time of day it will be, because I don't know for sure if I am stopping on the Panoramic-Express or just sitting on it for the whole journey. I don't fully understand exactly what's going to happen, but I will end up in Lucerne at some point. If my next destination is Venice, then I will need to travel through Italy, but which way? I also need to go as far as I can so that the next leg of the journey to Venice can be done in one day. There is a lot to think about and I make notes, maybe Lugano, or Como, or even Milan but I won't book anything yet.

Ljubljana is on my wish list of places to visit, but there's not a direct route from Venice and I don't have much experience on the scale of the map, so I am not sure how far everywhere is from each other. But that's the fun of it. I am really enjoying the planning side of this trip. Having my big Interrail map laid out on the table, studying it with the sun setting across Lake Geneva, is so surreal and exciting. I can honestly go anywhere that I want to, and that's a treat.

I put a post out on Facebook with some stunning photos, tidy all my maps and notebooks away, before going up to bed. I am super excited about the Panoramic-Express tomorrow.

The Panoramic-Express
Friday 7th August

If I had remembered that *escalier* was French for stairs, I would have got off at the right bus stop and possibly caught the 8.44 am Panoramic-Express. But the free bus ticket from the hostel did save me about 20 minutes of walking. It's just a shame that it didn't save me 30 and a steep walk up a hill with my bag.

I slept very well as the hostel was very quiet and my roommate was no bother. She didn't snore or get up and down in the night, in fact, I didn't really know she was there. It's still a strange concept being asleep, your most vulnerable time, and sharing your space with a complete stranger.

Breakfast was buffet style, laid out in a big room with lots of tables. There were quite a few people already in the room when I arrived. I had fruit, fruit juice, tea, delicious fresh bread, and even sunflower spread. I have always hated the taste of butter. I sneaked some bread with spread on out of the breakfast room and took a few extra portions of sunflower spread.

Now I have to wait 45 minutes for a train, and I am as excited as a three-year-old. It's not a bad station to wait at. It's good to breathe out and take it all in, instead of jumping straight on a train. This is an important day.

I can see Lake Geneva through the buildings and it's about 20°C already. I am wearing sunglasses at 9.15 am in the morning. I feel more in control today, even though I don't know where I am sleeping tonight. Yesterday I was a bit unsure of how to get out of Morzine, get a train to Montreux, and where to sleep. Now I have a little more confidence as yesterday worked out, so hopefully today will too. I have no concept of how long the Panoramic-Express is. I have a map which I picked up inside the train station. It's a wide picture of mountains and lakes and names that I don't recognise, but I can't put its size into context. I just know that I am so excited to be doing this after deciding during lockdown and here I am.

It's 9.26 am, and I am sitting on the train, very excited. You just never know what it's like to actually experience something rather than researching and reading about it and looking at photos that someone else took.

I am feeling a little anxious that I didn't buy a ticket, but the lady at the ticket booth said that I didn't need to. It seems as I look out of the window that people are holding reservations and looking for the right carriage to get in. I could be sitting in someone's seat and I have carefully chosen this one to be facing the right way and on the right side, as my research and the lady at the ticket office suggested. Fingers crossed that all is well.

The carriage has huge glass windows, not as much glass as I saw in a photo, but much bigger than a normal train. It feels light and airy with lots of blue sky. People are still rushing up and down the platform. It's now 9.44 am and I was told Swiss trains run like Swiss clocks. This train is one minute late but I can forgive them that and my seat is safe. I have not been turfed out.

Gosh, we are going up immediately. I have not done that on a train. We go through a dark tunnel and out again with wonderful views of Lake Geneva. This is going to be special.

Bye bye, Lake Geneva. We turn right, up into the mountains, I am guessing, but no, we are back out again. The lake is on my right this time. We must have done the equivalent of a hairpin bend on a train. We stop at Chernex, fingers crossed I don't lose my seat. No, I'm good and we move again.

Everyone in the carriage is quiet. There are five individual men spaced apart all over the carriage. The only sound is my camera going off, which is quite noisy. Lake Geneva is on my left again. This is so much fun. We go through another dark tunnel and then back to the mountains. The inspector has been and I haven't been thrown off. This amazing rail journey is included in my Interrail ticket which I think has been great value already.

I wasn't expecting so many stops or such big villages or hotels, schools, busy roads, and traffic. I thought it was just a scenic route. Isn't it funny how you picture something and it's nothing like it? What a place to live and work. Montbovon looks like a lovely place. In fact, it's all lovely. I am quite blown away by it.

Our carriage acquires three noisy French men holding see-through bags of fruit. I have to say I preferred the peace. I find I am trying to understand what they are saying, even though I don't want to. I only catch odd words as my French is rubbish, even though I passed my O-Level.

Château-d'Oex is another big town with pretty chalets. Then a field of parked gliders which I have never seen before. Liam had a friend stay in Morzine who brought his glider with him. He showed me the carpark that he parked it in. Some people live very different kinds of lives.

There are so many stops and people getting on and off, which isn't what I expected, I thought everyone on the train would be here for the entire journey of panoramic viewing. But I was very wrong. It's like a train going into London but with better scenery. That's not to say it's spoiling it. I just hadn't thought it would be like this. But that's what is so good about this trip, I have done such little research that everything is a surprise.

I just nipped to the toilet, and I am now eating a delicious plum that I bought in the Co-op last night for 80 francs, whatever that is; but it was worth it, it's sweet, juicy, and delicious.

I swap trains at Zweisimmen, which is very easy and quick. This train is more like a normal train but with fewer people and is perfectly comfortable. Now I am eating the bread that I took from breakfast.

We pass a huge great campsite full of motorhomes. Now that's an idea for another trip. We pass a few timber merchants with huge pine trees, trimmed and stacked in ginormous neat piles, ready to build more chalets.

I get off for an hour at Spiez at 1.33 pm. I wanted to stop somewhere and be in the beauty of Switzerland and I couldn't decide which was a good spot. The ticket lady at Montreux suggested here.

I am a little disappointed, and that sounds ridiculous if you could see the view that lies in front of me. Spiez looks beautiful. But I have severely underestimated how big these towns are. I thought I would get off the train and sit on a log or in a cute café, just there for people taking a break from the panoramic. That sounds ridiculous, but that's what I thought. Instead, I get off the train station at the top of a hill. The view is amazing, I mean, truly amazing. The colours of the sky and lake are incredibly blue, the grass is almost pastel green and with the backdrop of the mountains it's a picture-postcard view. But I can't get down to the lake, which is what I wanted to do. I hadn't thought about where the train station was in relation to the water, and I have messed up a little. I have messed up a lot. I am gutted that I can't get down to the edge of the water.

The harbour looks cute from what I can see so high up, but there is no way I am going to make it down with my backpack and definitely not back up again. I could get a taxi, but I don't have any currency. There are limited things that I can do now.

So, I take the next best option. I go into the supermarket café and buy tea, cake, and Coke, which costs me an absurd 10 francs, but I can pay on my card. There's a small seating area outside to take advantage of the view, so off I go with my tray and all my bags. People look at me like, 'Hope she's not sitting near me.'

I can't get the best seat next to the railings, but it's still a great view from my table. I tuck into my two drinks and cake. I have eaten more today than all of yesterday and it's still early. Someone starts to move and I collect my stuff. I am here for less than an hour and I want that seat by the railings with the uninterrupted view. So undiplomatically, I move my bags across before they have departed, but I don't care. There's no time for niceties today.

I sit in the spot that I wanted and stare down at the view and breathe out. Having the right seat is very important to me. I am in Switzerland and it's beautiful.

It's a lovely interlude with a stunning view and now it's time to get back on the train. I walk over to the train station, which is literally just across the road from the supermarket. People are talking German now, I think. I wasn't expecting that. I am a bit confused.

I get back on the train to Interlaken. It's only 20 minutes till I have to change trains again, but it will be efficient.

From the window Interlaken West looks lovely. I should have got off here, I could have got off here, and perhaps I wish I had. But maybe I will come back. On a canal there is a two-storey canal boat that probably came from the lake and lots of people milling about. It looks like a wonderful place to spend an afternoon, or maybe a week's holiday. This would have been a much better place to stop. I mustn't feel disappointed, at least I am here. I can see it's beautiful and I would feel confident coming back for a longer trip.

The onward journey is nothing short of stunning. The colours change, the water of the lake is turquoise, and the sky is a perfect blue against the dramatic backdrop of the mountains. The grass is a different colour than I have ever seen, lighter, with a hint of yellow and more vibrant. The whole colour palette here differs from anything that I have ever seen before and therefore I am struggling for words to describe it. There are houses and hotels on the edge of the lake with people swimming and sunbathing. It's possibly even more spectacular than I imagined. I absolutely must come back.

Brienz has to be the most beautiful train station that I have been to. The railings are right next to the water with a huge mountain framing the lake. I have run out of words to describe it. I would like to spend a week here, getting off at all the beautiful stops and staying in these hotels.

I take the photo that I have been trying to get for a while, out of the window with the train turning left so that the train is in the photo as well as the green grass and the mountains. It's one to frame. This is what I came Interrailing for; new experiences, new places, and new colours. I couldn't be happier right now.

I have to stop taking photos or I won't have memory on my SD card for the rest of the trip. I sit back and enjoy it, taking it all in. I am worn out from sensory overload.

And then it all ends and we change from scenic to built-up seamlessly, as we approach the city of Lucerne. The train station reminds me of approaching Liverpool Street station.

I get off feeling like I have just had an amazing experience and all these people don't know how happy and lucky I feel. The change in colours is confusing, my mind is full of vibrant greens, turquoise and blue, now it's all gone grey.

There are 20-plus platforms and thankfully a big screen to help me find my train to Lugano at 4.20 pm. I am not sure if I was supposed to reserve a seat. On the last train, I didn't.

This is such a contrast, and my brain is frazzled. I have just been through one of the world's most scenic places and now I am in commuter land, with thousands of bustling people, noise, life, and no scenery. And the beauty and nature is such a short ride away from here.

The doors are shut now, fingers crossed I don't need a ticket. It's a big train, so let's see what happens. It's a quiet carriage, a contrast to the train to Lucerne that filled up very quickly at the end after the scenery went away.

I need to make some decisions. I only have a very vague plan at the moment. I would like to have seen Lucerne, but it looks huge, judging by the buildings on the train track and the size of the station. That would have involved wandering around with my big heavy bag or staying there. If I stayed, I wouldn't have used my day's travel efficiently and I need to get a bit closer to Venice or I will need second day's travel. Lucerne to Venice is nine hours, which is way too far to travel in one day. So, if I travel a bit further now and find somewhere to sleep, I will hopefully get to Venice tomorrow. It's best to keep moving rather than wander aimlessly around a big city. I know that from Geneva. The backpack just gets heavier and heavier. I might come back as I certainly want to go on that Panoramic-Express again and stop a few times.

Maybe just travel there and back all day. That would make me very happy.

At 4.29 am, the ticket inspector comes by. He wants to see my ID, which is the first time that has happened, but I can sit back and chill now. Everyone is speaking Italian, the tannoy is Italian, I can't understand a word and we are still in Switzerland. I'm not sure why everyone is speaking Italian. It's now a two-hour train journey to Lugano.

Everywhere looks so flat, even though there are a few mountains in the distance. The colours are a bit quieter than they were on the Panoramic. But I am on my way to Italy now. I don't know where exactly and don't know where I am sleeping at the moment.

The landscape is dramatic at Flüelen with tall mountains on both sides, which are more rocky than pretty, and very dramatic.

Then it all goes dark. There's a digital display saying there is a tunnel 57km long but it's in Italian, then it comes up in English and I quickly take a photo. We are travelling through the Gotthard Base Tunnel. Wow, I wasn't expecting a world record tunnel that's 20 minutes long. It's weird to think we are in a tunnel right in the heart of a mountain.

Right, I need to find somewhere to stay. I switch on the data on my phone. There's a hostel in the centre of Como, that's a possibility. I could go to Milan, it's a bit further, and nearer to Venice. But it will be huge, so I don't fancy that. Mind you, I haven't googled Como yet, but it's not going to be as big as Milan, that's for sure and it has a lake.

I will aim for Como and the hostel. There is room at the moment on Booking.com. But I won't book it just in case I don't get that far.

We just passed a huge slate quarry and my neck hurts from looking up at all the mountains. I never thought that would happen. They are so much closer to the train than on the Panoramic and very solid and rocky.

There's a swift change of trains at Lugano at 18.35 pm. Gosh, it's hot out there. I have been on five air-conditioned trains today. It feels like Italy, but I don't think we have crossed into Italy yet.

The last train was brand new, swish, clean but this one is a bit older and very different, so it doesn't have a digital screen. It's a half-hour journey according to the Interrail app, so I need to concentrate so that I get off at Chiasso. There's another lake outside my window. I have seen so many lakes and mountains today.

At Chiasso, I get off the train, go through customs and onto the next train in six minutes. I didn't know that was possible. It's just a small station, but that still has to be a record, so now I must be in Italy.

The quality of the trains is deteriorating every time I change. This one has really old chairs, which are tatty and the carriage feels very dark. The doors don't open with flashy buttons; they need a lot of elbow effort to open them. I am also the only person in this old, dark carriage and I'm not that sure if I am in the right place as there's no way of knowing.

I feel uncomfortable, so I stand near the door and keep alert. It's only a five-minute journey. The next station is Como, I think. There are no signs hanging or on walls at the station as we pull in, so how am I supposed to know? I have to ask. I ask a lady getting onto the train in English as I don't know any Italian. I don't think she's impressed by this flustered English woman. But she gruffly says, 'Como,' so I get off. I eventually see a sign, so I am in the right place.

As I leave the train station there is a big sweeping set of steps to walk down. I screenshot the map to the hotel. A new tip for myself. Wi-Fi is very erratic, so I am taking a screenshot where I can and it's easier to follow than trying to get Wi-Fi and follow Google Maps and it saves my data. It's not far and I only go down one wrong road, which is pretty good for me.

The hostel looks OK from the outside. It's called Ostello Bello Lake Como Hostel. I can't decide whether to stop here for one or two nights. I will book one for now.

I enter through an iron gate off the road into an outdoor area with outdoor seats and tables, which are brightly coloured and have a Mediterranean feel. I wait patiently at the little desk in a cramped space at the bottom of the stairs while the man talks to the lady in front of me. It's all a little rustic, but it has a nice feel to it. A group of teenagers pass me as they come down the stairs and I feel very old.

I ask for a bed, knowing from the internet that there is one. The man assumes that this old woman doesn't do dorms and tells me there's a private room at the end of the courtyard and it's about €100. He is eyeing me up for a reaction. Am I a rich backpacker? If I was going to spend €100 on one night's accommodation, I would go to a hotel. I ask if there are any female dorms and he says he doesn't have any. This throws me a bit. In theory, I was OK with a mixed dorm from the safety of my home back in Cornwall. Back there it sounded OK, very Interrailing. But now, faced with the reality, I don't like the idea. It's 7.30 pm and I have travelled on the Panoramic-Express across Switzerland, on grotty trains across Italy, and I just need a bed, so I say yes. He says he'll put me on the bottom bunk. I feel a little put out. I have travelled across Europe on my own with this big backpack. Do I not look fit enough to climb a ladder? But actually I am relieved, it will be easier on a bottom bunk. Oh my god, what have I just agreed to?

I thank him and then he offers me earplugs which is not a good sign. He says the bar is open until 1.00 am and asks if I need shampoo. I really must wash my hair more often. I smile and tell him I have shampoo and earplugs. I don't say I am 55 years old, spent the lockdown researching my trip and I am old enough to know to that I should pack earplugs and shampoo?

The room is surprisingly OK. I have one roommate. He's not here, but his pants are hanging up to dry on the bed frame at the end of his bed. This is weird.

I lock my rucksack in the cupboard in the room and use the loo, an ensuite which I don't like. It's not like you can nip to the loo half-naked, so it might as well be outside so you don't turn the lights on and disturb people.

I decide to go straight out to explore, as it's getting late. I head for Lake Como, which is close by and the obvious place to visit first and it doesn't take long at all. The hostel is in a great spot, close to the train and the lake, but I am not stopping for two nights. I don't like the feel of the place. I can't explain why. The lake is OK, just a lake, this one doesn't bring out any positive emotions. I stroll around and the people don't look happy. They look suspicious. It feels like everyone is on edge a bit. I walk about for an hour. I need to eat, but the restaurants don't look inviting and I can't find a takeaway. I go to the mini supermarket next door to the hostel, buy a salad bowl and take it back to the hostel.

The room is still empty and I have a much-needed shower but skip the hair wash, as I don't want to go to sleep with wet hair.

I videocall Phil on Facebook. I am missing him and seeing him standing in his kitchen brings home straight back to me. But I knew this when I left. After saying goodbye, I take a moment to breathe out, and get on with journey planning. I am looking for a train to Venice and spend an hour researching loads of hotels. There are lots in Venice and I don't understand the layout or where any of them are. The better-priced ones seem to be a train ride away. I decided early on that I wasn't on an actual budget. Of course, I don't want to be frivolous, but picking a well-placed hotel is paramount. I enjoy picking hotels, so it's not a chore. It's very relaxing and exciting.

My roommate turns out to be a French man of about 35. He comes in while I am researching Venice. He is very pleasant, which is a relief. I am lying in my bed when he comes in, which is a strange way to meet a new person. He shuts the floor-to-ceiling windows, and it takes a while because they are old and have a strange, old locking system and wooden shutters. We speak for about five minutes, just to be polite, we are sharing a bedroom after all. Then he says he is going to sleep. Brilliant. Perfect. I put my little bed light on and he turns the room light off.

He is on the bottom of the bunk next to me, our feet meeting – which is as good as we are going to get in the room full of bunk beds. I carry on searching for a hotel in Venice and book two nights. After this I message my friend Angela. We had recently got back in touch after not talking for a while. It was a strange situation because I didn't like her husband and she didn't like mine. So, we sort of parted ways and she moved up north from Harlow, and I moved to Cornwall from Harlow. But I am very happy that we are talking again and so I message her about my trip so far and then turn off my light.

How easy was that? This mixed dorm stuff is OK. I am spending the night with a man that I have never met before, but at least he wants to sleep and not party.

Then at 11.00 pm, just as I am drifting off to sleep, our new roommate noisily bundles through the door. He turns on the room light and opens the shutters and windows that the French man spent ages shutting without even uttering a word or asking if it is OK. As you know, this is my first mixed dorm, so I am not sure what the etiquette is, but it feels rude. Then he goes for a shower in our little bathroom. I think he is having a full exfoliating session as he is taking ages. Back in the room he starts rearranging his bags and he has no concept that he is disturbing us. The French man is sighing with irritation but it is far too subtle.

The music and people downstairs are getting louder as they drink more. We have missed our opportunity to get to sleep. There is a traffic light outside on a busy junction, so we have engines revving, adding to the mix.

Eventually, our roommate falls asleep and starts snoring loudly.

Lake Como to Venice
Saturday 8th August

I get up at 7.45 am, pack quickly and go downstairs for the free tea and orange juice. The tea is awful and I can't drink it. I didn't know it was possible to make tea that bad. I pop into the mini supermarket next door and buy another salad bowl. Yesterday's was very good and it's easy to eat. I also get a freshly baked bread roll for my train journey.

An elderly lady is begging as I walk towards the wide steps leading up to the station. It is more like a performance, with dramatic gestures and some kind of wailing. She is leaning over a stick and the only word I can make out is *bambino*, but she looks about 100 years old. I look behind me and there is no one else around. The performance is all for my benefit. I don't have any currency even if I wanted to give her anything, so I drop my eyes and walk past quickly.

I am on the train at 9.19 am. It's an old train, with plastic-covered seats and a dirty floor. We have definitely left the cleanliness of Switzerland behind now. I have to change in Milan which I am not looking forward to, it's going to be crazy. I think I have to go on the Underground and get across to another station. Like going into London and arriving at Paddington and then getting across to Liverpool Street station. Not always easy in your own country and I don't speak Italian.

So, I sit back on the tatty chairs and look at the graffitied trains across the platform. I am starving as I only had a salad bowl for tea last night. I don't want to open my salad bowl now as everything looks dirty. I butter the bread that I bought in the shop with the sunflower spread that I still have from Montreux. The bread is delicious but chewy. I let that go down and digest before I eat any more.

The view out of the window is not great, every station seems to have graffiti. It feels poor and uncared for.

At the station, the digital display says my train is at platform 20. So, I go to platform 20, and there is no one there. I have to be brave now and talk to someone. One lady can't understand me, we just can't communicate, so I say thanks and move away. The platform is totally empty, except for a cleaner with a big brush and trolley. I will have to ask him. His English is not good either, but better than my Italian, which is nothing. I have written the name of my destination down on a piece of paper. It's my new way of trying to interact with people. It's a much swifter way of communicating when you can't pronounce the destinations.

My new system works. The man knows what I am asking for. Result. I feel back in control a bit. It's much easier to ask people as you don't have to pronounce the word and it's easy to check the time and trains.

He manages to explain that the '20' means the train is 20 minutes late, not the platform number. This is obviously why no one is here as it's the wrong platform. I have learnt now that on the display boards for trains 'BIN' means binary, which is platform, and 'RIT' means your train is going to be late. Because my train is late, there is no platform number yet. So, I decide to go to the middle one. When the number is announced, I can go left or right. You can see across the platforms and there is a tunnel to get to the others.

As it turns out, I am on the right one and I am very relieved to see the train. This has been the only delay so far on the trip, and it wasn't much at all.

I swap trains at Milan. It's an easy transfer, and this train is packed and there are no seats available. You would never know there is a pandemic going on if it weren't for the masks. I stand in the corridor by the doors, as there is no room in the carriage. But these are pretty full too. There is no social distancing, so I turn and face the window to create my own little space and look out of the window. I put my big bag on the floor, tucking it into the corner out of everyone's way, and hover over it. I have a great view out of the window of the passing, dirty and unkept platforms, with weeds everywhere, graffiti, and a complete lack of love and care.

I am not feeling Italy. I hope Venice is not like this. Every time the door opens, I breathe in some fresh air. It's as warm on the platforms as it is on the train, but it is new air, not recycled like on the train. I am not getting cross, though. I am on an adventure and this bit is a little difficult. I am lucky to be doing the journey at all.

I stand by the doors for two hours, melting in the heat.

As we get close to my station, Verona Porta Nuova, where I need to change, people are on their phones. I guess because we were late, people's connections are tight. My train is not due for an hour and seven minutes, so I step aside and let them all fly off the train.

I find a digital display and I look up and it seems there is a train to Venice soon. So I walk, I can't run with this backpack on. I see the train doors are about to close and two girls jump on. I look at the screen again. It says, 'Venice S l.'

In a split second, I decide to jump on. It's a risk.

This train is new, nothing like the old one that I just got off. It has a digital screen, so I can immediately see that I am heading to Venice. All is good. I am chuffed that I had the confidence to get on it. I am on my way to Venice and I saved an hour which makes me very happy. Who wouldn't want to have an extra hour in Venice? It's like the clocks going back, a bonus hour.

I am now super excited, and my hotel looks great on paper. Let's hope all my research has paid off.

The scenery is improving, which is encouraging. Green flat fields and tiny houses, terracotta rooftops. We seem to have left behind the graffiti and general disarray of the last squished train journey. The flats that we pass have flowers on the balcony instead of washing. There are flower displays instead of weeds on the stations. I must sound like a snob and I am really not. I was raised on a council estate in Harlow, Essex, and am proud of it. I think I am picking up on the feeling of a place rather than whether they have time to garden.

But we still have a beggar on board, handing out tatty, handwritten letters to everyone. They're dog-eared and well used, possibly never even been read. After walking the length of the carriage, he returns for them and I don't see anyone give him any money, just his bits of paper. It's an unusual tactic of begging and doesn't seem to be working for him. I actually want to give him some money, but I don't have any Italian change.

It isn't a long journey to Venice and very easy and I get more excited the closer we get.

The train goes over an expanse of water on a narrow piece of land, just wide enough for the railway tracks, which makes it feel like you are entering somewhere special. I can see the buildings of Venice over the water as the train slows down.

Then we are in Venice. It feels like a holiday destination, like going to the seaside on the train. Southend or Clacton come to mind, reaching the end of the line.

I step off the train and walk out of the station, straight into a picture postcard of Venice. The train station is metres from the first canal. So, Venice hits you immediately. I just stand in awe. I am here. I am in Venice and it looks amazing. It is so vast and wide and clean and stunning, I can't take it all in. There's a church of some kind with a big green dome, like a mini St Paul's Cathedral. On the other side, brick buildings and a big bridge over the canal. It's just like on the TV. I love it already and I wasn't sure that I should even come here.

I know almost nothing about Venice, except what I have seen on the television. I don't know how big it is, or what's here. I just know it has lots of canals and gondolas. I am so excited to go and explore.

I go over the huge bridge. It's a little bit of a struggle with my backpack, but a whole lot easier than with a suitcase. I watch someone ahead of me trying to lift the wheels of their suitcase up the steps, whereas I just need to concentrate on finding my footing.

I find my way to the hotel. It's just 10 minutes' walk and, by god, it's hot.

The hotel is perfect, right on a canal. Mind you, it would be hard not to be on or near a canal from what I have seen so far. But it looks amazing. It's called Hotel Al Sole. It's four storeys high and made of red brick with ornate windows.

I stand out the front of the hotel for a moment and take it all in. It's so picturesque. The water in the canal is still, there are skinny boats moored, and gondolas, many with cloth covers on, all tied up outside buildings. The buildings are tall, three or four storeys high and they all look old and full of character. It's warm, and the sky is blue and without a cloud. I love it here already and I was nervous that it wouldn't be my kind of place, too touristy, but it's beautiful.

I check in. My room doesn't look over the canal, but it has a perfectly nice view down on the hotel courtyard, full of flowers and a few iron tables and chairs. The hotel is perfect and it has a nice feel, the staff are lovely and it feels very old and full of character. It's 15th century, which is why I booked it. I love hotels with character and I wanted a treat after the hostels.

I have a much-needed shower and pack my small bag with a map the receptionist gave me and my camera. I asked the receptionist where I could fill up my water bottle and she looked a little confused and told me to fill it up in the toilet sink, which I now do.

Then I walk out of the hotel and straight over the bridge outside the hotel door. I wander about, over bridges, along narrow lanes with tall buildings where you can hardly see the sky, then open bits, more bridges, more canals, and I get completely lost. There is hardly anyone around and I am not sure if that's because there is a pandemic on, or because I am totally lost.

I stop to look at my map. It turns out that I am near the ferry port and not in the heart of things. I have drifted away from the heart of Venice to the edge and I can see the open sea. I am basically lost and very tired now, having been on stuffy trains all day, and I am so thirsty.

I take a drink of water from my bottle, water from the toilet sink, but it doesn't feel right. It's a shame, as I am very thirsty, but I don't want to be ill. I turn back into the streets and see a few more people and small bridges again, which is a relief. There, in front of me, in an outside area next to an intersection of bridges and canals, is a drinking spot. I collapse into a chair. An absolutely perfect spot to watch the world go by. My legs need to sit down as they have been standing for two hours on the train.

I look at the menu, and lemon soda pops out. Just what I need, so I order one of those and a fizzy water as I don't think they give out free tap water here. I am extremely thirsty, a little dehydrated from the hot train and lack of liquid today.

The lemon soda is like nectar; cold, fizzy, zingy, and the best thing I have drunk in ages. I sit at this cute outdoor table, sheltered by a tree, and take in the fact that I am in Venice. I really can't believe it. Boats are going up and down the canal, small speed boats and gondolas. A real-life gondola just sailed past me and I can't help smiling. This is exactly what I wanted to get out of this trip, moments like this. I almost have to pinch myself.

The buildings are beautiful; all different colours: mustard, dusky pink, burnt orange, pale orange. The restaurants all have flowers outside. Venice is beautiful. It would be a great place to come if you enjoyed painting. There are so many colours, beautiful buildings and gently rippling water in the canals. I could stay in this very spot for days and days.

I can feel myself exhaling. It's been such a busy week, and I have seen so much, from Morzine in France to Lake Geneva, the Panoramic-Express, Como, sketchy Italy and now I am here in Venice, for two nights. I am so lucky.

My gut feeling was that I would enjoy travelling on my own, as I am perfectly happy in my own company, but I could have been wrong.

My whole life I have felt alone, even when I wasn't. I can't really explain it. I don't interact well with people unless I know them very well. I was so different from my brother and sister, so I didn't form any deep bonds there. My dad left to marry someone else and my mum was so very busy trying to work and keep a roof over our heads. I have travelled through life alone and I am used to my own company. So, I am enjoying this trip. It feels natural sitting here in Venice on my own. I am free to choose where I sit and where I go and I love it.

Once refreshed, I decide to move on and explore some more. I walk over bridges, around corners, across little squares, up narrow lanes. I take many photos; every time I turn a corner, there is another photo to take. People are everywhere, pausing on the tiny bridges, trying to take their own photos of Venice.

I find a much wider canal. It's as wide as a motorway, but it's water and has boats and gondolas going down instead of cars. It's quite busy. There are lots of wooden poles outside the big buildings to secure your boat. I am blown away by the beauty of it. It's very old, the buildings magnificent, and lining the canal so beautifully. People live and work here, parking their boats just like we park our cars on the street at home.

Soon, I am lost again. I pass a chocolate shop for the second time, but I don't care. I am loving every corner that I turn, every bridge that I cross.

By now, I am really hungry, searching for something to eat, and it's all Italian; pizza, pasta, meatballs, and spaghetti. I want a nice spot to sit and eat. When you eat on your own, it's important to have a nice view as you won't be talking to anyone. I have a picture in my mind of Jamie when he came to Venice. In his photo, he is sitting by the canal eating dinner. I want to find something similar.

I stop at a cute restaurant with a single row of seats, right next to a canal. This is what I've been looking for. I order a mushroom pizza, which is not vegan which is what I prefer to eat, but I am in Venice, on a trip of a lifetime, so I want to try a real Italian pizza. It's that simple.

The little Italian man in the restaurant makes a fuss over me, bringing me my drink and napkins. This is such a great spot next to the water. The sun is just going down, but it's still lovely and warm. When it arrives, the pizza is delicious, hot, and freshly made, the mushrooms perfectly cooked. It is very satisfying.

Afterwards, I walk back to my hotel. It takes some finding, as my map doesn't make any sense to me. Back in my lovely room in my lovely hotel, I feel tired and very happy. My app says that I walked six miles today in Venice, which explains why I am shattered.

I have another shower and ring Phil. He says he was worried about me last night in the mixed dorm and was happy to get the text earlier saying that I was OK. I must remember how important my texts and messages home are. I message some people, put a post on Facebook, and chill for a bit. It's so nice to think I am not rushing off tomorrow.

Venice
Sunday 9th August

I wake to the sound of bells ringing, which has to be the most perfect way to wake up in Venice. I make a cup of green tea with the kettle I acquired at reception yesterday. If you don't ask, you don't get. I have my own loose green tea with me, in one of those tiny glass jam pots you get at hotels. I drink green tea every morning at home, to wake me up, and then I move on to builder's tea. On this trip, I drink my green tea at every opportunity, as there isn't any proper tea anywhere. Having a kettle in my room makes me feel warm and fuzzy, and homely. I can now make a cup of green tea whenever I want.

I have a shower and wash some clothes in the sink, before hanging them on the little railings of my window. I think they will be dry by the end of the day, especially in this heat. I lay out my map of Venice on the double bed and look at the island I am on. I missed St Mark's Square yesterday, even though I saw signposts for it. Before coming here, I had done very little research on Venice – practically no research at all, as I wasn't in a big hurry to visit. I don't know what it's all about, but I will go and have a look. So that's my plan after breakfast.

Breakfast is a weird COVID-19 one. The breakfast buffet looked incredible when I was researching this hotel, but all the hotels are trying to keep everyone safe, so I fully understand. I sit at a chair and table in the courtyard, one I can see from my bedroom window, and I choose some items off a sheet of paper to tell the staff what I would like for breakfast.

It's not a great breakfast for a vegan/veggie, but they are doing their best, and I am struggling to communicate with the waitress. I bet the buffet before COVID-19 restrictions was amazing. Instead, the pear I am given is rock hard, so I have bread and sunflower spread with a little cheese. I have declined all the meat options and a boiled egg, so there's not much left. I do feel bad eating cheese, but I have to eat something.

I put my tracker on and step out of the hotel into the heat. It's 10.30 am and I wasn't expecting it to be this hot already. Today, I am going to enjoy myself, I have all day to explore. I bought a selfie stick in Truro especially for the trip, and I have only just taken it out of the box this morning. I feel a little silly, as I don't even know how it works. I am camera shy and, being old and wrinkly, I don't ever take selfies. I don't normally want photos of myself, but this is a trip of a lifetime and I want some photos of me in Venice and other places.

I have brought two phones with me in case I lose one, but today I have both in my bag, so that's a bit daft. The second one has my new selfie stick attached to it.

I get to the first pretty bridge, well, prettier than some, as they are *all* pretty. I self-consciously get my selfie stick out with the camera dangling off the end and try to take a photo. It's a very cheap selfie stick, meaning I can't open it too far as it won't hold the weight of my phone.

Discreetly, in the corner of the gorgeous, very small bridge (and still feeling silly), I take a few photos. Immediately, I can see what they look like. I laugh at how hideous I look and try again. I should have put some eyeliner on, I should have taken them a bit further back, so it looks like I have fewer wrinkles, or a bigger smile, and maybe I should lose the floppy hat. Gosh, I do look old and I do feel silly, which isn't helping. It seems odd smiling at my camera when there's no one else here but that's the whole point of a selfie, I suppose. I put it back in my bag, laugh at myself, and move on. I have embarrassed myself enough in this spot. The bridge is small and busy and probably not the best spot to learn how to take a selfie. I laugh again as I walk off. I should have asked Tami for a lesson as she takes great selfies.

I soon pass what's called the Rialto Bridge going over the Grand Canal. Nearby, there are signs on the tall buildings pointing to more bridges. I walk up onto the Rialto and look down, realising I can walk down to the edge of the water and take a photo where it's quieter, with the bridge in the background. It's very busy up here with lots of people coming and going, both ways, while many stop to take photos of the view and themselves. It's a bit chaotic. There are fewer people down by the water, and I am getting the hang of my new gadget. I take some half-decent photos of myself. That's a first.

St Mark's Square is huge, especially after all the tiny lanes. It's such a contrast. There is a very large, ornate cathedral at one end, St Mark's Basilica. I try to photograph it but there's a stall of tat in front of it. You'd think whoever was in charge would make them pitch it to the side.

The square is lined on three sides by long rows of three-storey buildings, very ordered, formal looking, and imposing, especially compared to the irregular feel of the canal buildings. This feels like an important square and it's almost empty, maybe because of COVID-19. There was a programme on television recently saying how much Venice has benefitted from the lack of tourism, and that the canals are now much cleaner. I am honoured to be here at this special time.

I know absolutely nothing about the history of where I am standing or why it is here. I need to do some research as I know I am missing a layer to my trip by not having this background information. But, even so, I can feel its importance, and enjoy it for what it is. I don't necessarily need to know all the details to appreciate how spectacular it is.

In the corner is a tall brick tower and I think about going up. I bet the views across the island and canals are amazing. There is a queue outside, but it doesn't look that long, especially when it might be a mile long in normal times. I am very tempted to join, but decide to stay on the ground, choosing not go up inside any buildings or on the water. I simply don't have time to do it all. Hopefully, I will come back with Phil one day, and we can do some more exploring.

I wander around the edge of the island that is Venice, and I am at open water now. I can see another island, Isola della Giudecca, my map says. I would love to have gone over there, and also to Murano to see the glassblowing. There is such a lot to do here.

It feels different at the edge next to the open water. The air is fresher and the streets are much wider, with deep pavements between the buildings and the water's edge. I think if I had stayed here, in this part of Venice, I would have had a very different time to being in the heart of the canals. It makes a nice change to the tiny lanes. Venice is a very varied place with a unique colour palette. That's one thing I have noticed from my trip so far, that each place has its own colour palette. Morzine was lush green with pine lodges. Montreux featured blue water, blue sky, and green foliage along the promenade. The Panoramic had a colour palette sent down from heaven. And now Venice is beige, terracotta, dusky pink, and white stone, with deep blue water. It's the colour of pizza on a blue plate.

I look for somewhere to get a drink by a canal, wandering over bridges that meet the open water, and end up turning back onto tiny lanes again, past a military-looking place which I wasn't expecting, and pause on a pretty bridge. Just over the small canal, there is a cute restaurant with hanging baskets and bright flowers, right next to the water. There's a seat waiting for me if I can get there quick enough. I find a spot with a view of another church tower. Apparently, there are about 100 churches on this island part of Venice, 150 canals, and about 400 bridges. I did a little bit of research last night on why there are so many canals and bridges because I wanted to know a bit more. There's a lot of information about how the island was built, by putting wooden poles deep into the mud. It sounds impossible to me, but here I am.

I order another lemon soda and an extra glass of ice, ready to sit and chill. It's good to stop moving and relax, and just take it all in. It's beautiful here. Flowers bloom in little baskets at my side, a canopy shading me to keep the intense heat away, but I still enjoy the warmth. The church sits on the other side of the little bridge, while people stroll by as boats glide up and down the water. Another idyllic spot, the cold drink, and rest is very welcome.

The waiter kindly points out where I am on my map because I have no idea. And then a man with an accordion at the restaurant next door starts playing beautiful music. I couldn't be happier. What are the chances of that happening? There are so many layers to Venice, the visuals, the heat, the cooler water at the edge, the smell of pizza cooking, and now music.

Once my drink is finished, I decide to move on. I am trying to get the balance between chilling and exploring. Now that I know where I am, at least for the moment, I am going to try and reach the yellow district on my colour coordinated map. I am heading for Cannaregio, which is right at the edge of the island on the other side, nearer the train station.

In the end, I sort of go the way I wanted to. There are lots of left and right decisions to make. It's more open here with wider streets, which are less pretty, with fewer people and hardly any restaurants. I reach the sea where it's even more vast. I can see the train track back to the mainland now, so I know exactly where

I am, which is a novelty. Soon, I turn a corner into a wide canal, Canale di Cannaregio, which goes into the main Canal Grande.

Admittedly, I am a bit worn out with decision-making since getting to Venice. In any new place that you visit, you learn where you are by travelling around and getting to know the streets but, here, it's almost impossible. I haven't had a sense of knowing where I am very often. It feels like I have constantly been lost. In this area, I do occasionally see a landmark, like a chocolate shop or big sweet shop that I have seen already, but that just means I have been lost on this street already. It isn't any help. I have seen so many people standing on bridges and street corners, looking up and down, staring at street signs on the walls and being none the wiser as the signs don't match their maps. I work out the main bridges on the Grand Canal are on the walls, so you know roughly in which area you are, but not exactly.

Right now, I am about 10 minutes from my hotel as I am back near the train station. I see a café with tables outside next to a wider canal, and my tummy is rumbles. I take a quick peep at the menu for offerings and prices before sitting down. I order a large bottle of fizzy water – no more lemon soda, I can feel it rotting my teeth – so I can take what I don't drink back to my room. I also order a salad and a bowl of fried tempered veg. It's just what speaks to me on the menu.

I take another selfie. It's going to be amusing looking at these back at the hotel.

The food is perfect. Hot deep-fried tempered veg, which is probably from a frozen bag, but that's OK, it's hot and scrummy. The salad is lovely too. It's pleasant here watching all the water activities; I am opposite a water bus stop. People are queuing as you would for a bus, and I watch them getting on and off. I haven't the courage or the time to try that. But I am happy to watch the comings and goings over my lunch.

My tracker says that I have walked 5.69 miles. No wonder my legs ache and I am hungry. It's 2.22 pm. Wow, the time has flown and all I have done is walk and look at views. I have a better feel for Venice now, despite getting lost.

I go back to the hotel and rest for a couple of hours. I am shattered and hot from the heat. The tracker is great as it shows me where I have been, which is amusing because it is not quite where I planned to go, but not too bad either, considering there are no straight roads or proper signposts.

After my rest, I go out again for my last proper stroll around Venice. There are lots of shops, whole streets of them, in this area. But I am not buying anything because I will have to carry it in my rucksack the rest of the trip. I don't need anything that badly. I have enough memories and photos to remind me of my trip.

I don't like shopping much anyway, so it's not a problem. When I was a teenager, I went into town one Saturday with my friends. I hated it. Standing around in a group of about six, looking at my friends pick up clothes from rails. I never really understood what was happening, and I didn't go again. It's a complete waste of time. Watching other people decide whether to buy a pink or blue top. Shopping is a necessity when I need a gift for someone or a new pair of leggings. Unless it's craft stuff. I love craft shops and charity shops, but I prefer to shop on my own, so that I can think properly.

Maybe that's why I have enjoyed travelling solo as I don't need to ask anyone else if they are OK. Are they happy, or enjoying themselves? Do they want to eat here, or there? It means I can be totally relaxed and free.

I buy a donut and a bottle of water before reluctantly turning back for the hotel. This trip to Venice is almost finished.

I make a cup of tea with my kettle and eat the donut, message Phil and put some photos on Facebook. Then I take a shower and book a hostel in Ljubljana in Slovenia for two nights. The hotels are at least €50 a night when the hostel is only €66 for two nights – in a private room, including breakfast, which sounds perfect. That's a saving of €34 and the only difference is that I don't have a private bathroom.

I plan tomorrow's train journey. The trains are hourly to Trieste and I'll need a bus after that to reach Ljubljana, which I don't like the idea of, but can't seem to avoid. I am excited about seeing Ljubljana and being in Slovenia. It sounds like an interesting place, not somewhere I ever thought of going to.

I have loved Venice. It's huge, much bigger than I imagined, more complicated, more stunning ... just *more*. Apart from the canals and bridges, there are some huge buildings, chunky heavy ones that I can't believe haven't sunk into the water. After more research, I discover that the wooden platforms and stone bring together 118 islands into what is now Venice, and it's 1,200 years old.

It's a truly amazing place and I will treasure my memories here.

Venice to Ljubljana
Monday 10th August

I wake early as it's not so easy to relax on a travel day. I consider skipping breakfast as it's not great if you don't eat meat and wonder if I should catch the 7.39 am train, before deciding there's not much point. I might as well go and eat whatever is on offer.

I leave the hotel at 8.17 am after paying the tax and for water I drank out of the fridge, and step out onto a warm street. Nearby, people are arriving on a small boat while their luggage is being taken off with a small crane which is unusual.

It's a 10-minute walk to the station and I am loaded again with all my bags, so I don't bother with the map. It's straightforward; right at the end of this canal, then right again where I should see the station. After 20 minutes and passing the same building twice, however, I admit defeat. It should have taken 10 minutes; it's a million degrees Celsius and now I am cross with myself for not using the map after all. I am not sure what I did wrong, but my back and shoulders are hurting, and I don't know where I am.

The problem with Venice is that there are a lot of similar looking walls from tall buildings. It's quite dense in places, and you often get to the end of a lane where in front of you, is a building, then you have to turn left or right, even though you want to go straight. Then this happens again, and again, and before you know it, you don't even know which direction you are facing.

I sit down on some church steps that I have walked past already, take my bag off for some relief, and switch on my data. When I get going again, I leave Google Maps on until I get to the station and arrive at 8.56 am, having missed the 8.39 am.

I need to nip to the loo, but there is a queue and a fee of €1.00. I don't think you should have to pay at a train station, so I don't go, and cross my legs instead.

The 9.39 am train leaves on time and I go straight for a wee before sitting down. I feel a bit sad leaving Venice as it was so much fun and exceeded my expectations on every level. Hopefully, one day, I will return.

I text Phil to say I am on the train to Trieste and he says, according to the fridge door, I am on schedule, but he doesn't know what's happening after Ljubljana. I forgot I had left my vague plan on the door. It makes me smile, as I don't know what's after Ljubljana, either. I close my eyes for a bit, which is the first time I have done that on these trains but the view out of the window is back to graffiti, so flat and dull. I am not that impressed with Italy, outside of Venice.

We get off at Monfalcone to swap onto a bus and it goes OK, despite my big bag. As we approach Trieste, I see out of the right-hand window lots of people swimming in the sea. The bus then follows the vast expanse of water into Trieste. I've heard it is nice here on the Interrail Facebook page. But you can't go everywhere. I did consider it, even for one night, before I booked my trip, but I am excited to go to Ljubljana.

The bus drops us at the train station in Trieste. A kind lady tells me the next bus to Ljubljana is at 2.00 pm, an hour and a half's time. While I wait, I sit in the park and eat the banana roll from breakfast, then take a slow stroll along the main road to find the water. I don't go too far with my backpack on, passing powerful, imposing, and ornate buildings. Someone on the Interrail page said they came here by chance and it was the favourite place of their trip. Even from this brief visit, I can see why. Everything here feels clean and organised, impressive and safe. The sea is vast and huge. When I remember the map in my head and work out where I am, it all makes sense. There's a ferry terminal here too. I am not sure where it goes, probably back to Venice and down to Croatia. I wouldn't mind arriving here by ferry and enjoying what Trieste has to offer.

I am melting on the short walk back to the bus station, walking slowly with my bag hurting my shoulders. I am dripping with the heat. It was difficult but I am glad I walked to the ferry terminal and got a feel of where I am. It's such a big place. You just can't tell from a map and a few photos sometimes.

When I arrive back, the bus station café is cool and I can sit down comfortably here until my bus arrives. I have water with me, but it tastes hot enough to bathe in. They have lemon soda in the fridge by the till, so that's an easy decision, plus a nice surprise. Cold and fizzy and zingy. A little unexpected treat to cool me down.

I should be in Ljubljana by 4.00 pm. The hostel is close to the train station, so hopefully it's not too much further arriving by bus.

The bus ride to Ljubljana is a treat, and I am so excited. Liam, Aidan, and Ciara went here on their Interrail trip and enjoyed it. They all said it was really pretty. The wiggly climb out of Trieste is dramatic and stunning, with amazing views across the huge landscape, right on the edge of the vast sea.

Slovenia is lovely, with green mountains off into the distance, and a great road system. The houses are all painted white or pale colours with fancy terracotta roofs. The language on signposts and adverts is strange with lots of J's, V's, and Z's. The language that I can hear on the bus is very different from Italian.

The roads are empty along these hairpin bends and the bus driver is doing a great job. I have no idea when I am coming into Ljubljana, but the scenery is pretty. English songs play on the bus radio. It's funny, all the countries I have been to play English songs, which is so odd when you are not even sure where you are.

Gentle green hills stretch outside my window now, with mountains and fir trees again, tall and straight. All the houses are pretty, with lots of flowers. We have just travelled through a place called Planina. There are miles of green fields, no apparent boundaries, just ambling fields. I didn't see much greenery in Venice, so this is a contrast. We are passing lots of little white churches with terracotta tile roof tiles that look sweet. One is very tiny.

I feel like I am in a different country, which is a silly thing to say, but it feels different and unfamiliar. Slovenia is a country that I don't know anything about. I only recently found out where it is on the map.

Now we have just passed through Vrhnika, a bigger town. The English language filters into everything here. A delivery van is parked outside the window of the bus, on the road next to me, with, 'In time,' written amongst the Slovenian writing.

We approach Ljubljana, and the pretty green towns disappear. I am a bit confused because it's getting busier with traffic. Ljubljana is much bigger than I thought it was going to be. It's not at all pretty and looks very unkempt and dirty. The roads are being dug up, there are tatty-looking flats and lots and lots of graffiti.

Oh dear.

The bus pulls into a bus station and everyone gets off. I look around. Surely we are not here, it looks awful. The children promised me a pretty photographic place, and the Interrailing community said you must stop here.

The driver stands up and looks at me. I am the only person left on the bus and he says, 'Ljubljana'. So, reluctantly, I get off. I pause and use Google to find my hostel. It says my hostel is 10 minutes away, so I am in the right place, unfortunately. I trot along the graffiti-lined streets, feeling uneasy.

The hostel looks OK from the outside, which is a plus, and the lady at reception speaks English, which is a relief. It's called Hostel Tabor, Ljubljana. The building feels like a prison, not necessarily in a bad way. It has long corridors, tall ceilings, and tiled floors. After checking in, I climb four flights of stairs, two on each floor, to my room. It's hard work with my backpack on. Each landing is the same with the long, straight, plain corridors. When I get to my door, it's huge, but once inside my room, it feels like student accommodation. There are two beds; luckily the lady at reception assured me I am not sharing. The room is narrow, the beds at far ends. I choose the one near the window as it has more light. Two desks stand against the right-hand wall, with cupboards on the left. It's perfect really, especially as I have it all to myself. It feels safe and comfortable.

I shower quickly in the bathroom across the wide hallway. It takes me a while to find a showerhead that will hang up and produce warm water. I then pack a bag and go out as I am desperate to find somewhere pretty I can take photos of.

I have to pass so much graffiti that it's annoying me and dragging me down. Outside one house is a young boy of about three or four and I watch him run back indoors. The entire house is covered in graffiti, with no room left to write anything else. The shops and alleyways are all touched with graffiti too. It's horrible – not nice, arty graffiti but scrawls of words and tags in black, red, or blue paint. I am finding it quite disrespectful. Some of these buildings look old and full of character, and yet they have been attacked with spray cans.

After a 10-minute walk, I arrive at a green bank of grass with trees lining the river. I start taking photos, strolling up one side of the river over a bridge and back down the other side. I see lots of lovely, impressive buildings and pretty scenes. There are seating areas down by the water, and people are sitting with friends, drinking wine from bottles. The pavements are full of tables and chairs from restaurants and I am hungry but can't see anything I want to eat. Nearly all the boards outside the restaurants are written in Slovenian, so I can't read them anyway.

I walk back. Near the hostel, I see a mini market so buy a pot of hummus and crisps. I want a cold cider or fizzy water, but there is only beer and Coke in the fridge, so I sadly go without.

I return to my room and feel a bit deflated. I don't like it here. Whether that's because I am tired or just come from Venice, I don't know. Maybe my expectations were too high, and it just didn't line up. Maybe I haven't seen the best bits yet. But I am definitely feeling a bit bleurgh. It's the first low point of the whole trip, except for that tough two-hour squashed train journey on the way to Venice. But this is different, and it comes after such a high.

I am questioning why I am here. What do I want to get out of this trip? I have seen so many amazing things that I could go home now and be perfectly happy. I have had so much fun already. Maybe a month is too long on your own, travelling such long distances.

I really don't know.

I phone Phil, he has hiccups from eating his dinner too fast and it makes me smile. I miss him.

I ring Ciara, and she sends me photos of her trip to Ljubljana. I didn't see any of those places when I went out just now. Mind you, I was only out an hour and a half. She also says maybe I should move on, that's what Interrailing is all about. If you don't like somewhere, move on. I contact Aidan and he is confused that I haven't seen any pretty bits. He sends me photos as well and says that he loved Ljubljana. So, I can't have seen it all yet.

I talk to Liam, and he says that he's had a great day out on the mountains with friends. I can picture him now that I have been to Morzine. I also know when he says he has been up a mountain, he really means he has been up a mountain, and I hope he stays safe. He suggests I go on the walking tour tomorrow, which I had thought about, after seeing a leaflet in reception. He also recommends I go up to the castle. I did see a vegan café on my walk, which was shut as it's the evening, but it looked good, so I should enjoy that. Food always makes me happy.

I go down four flights of stairs to the kitchen to make a cup of green tea. There's no one around, so much for making new friends or simply mingling and exchanging stories. After all that walking, I am very thirsty and it's a long way back to the top, so I make two cups of tea. I ignore the sign on the door about removing cups from the kitchen and take them back to my room. While eating my hummus and crisps, I study the map that was given me and plan a few things.

I need to go to sleep and wake up in a better mood so I can go out and explore. Then, tomorrow, think about how to get to Lake Bled, which I have decided is my next major stop.

Ljubljana
Tuesday 11th August

I slept well last night, eventually, after the French lad next door finished watching his film.

Once I'm ready for this morning, I head downstairs for the free breakfast in hopes of socialising, although I am not a natural socialiser. In fact, I hate social situations, I always have done. I am a very awkward person and worry about what I should or shouldn't say. I wasn't brought up in a social household, so I didn't learn many skills. But I am in a hostel in Ljubljana, one of the hot spots for Interrailing and as I walk across the grass, I psyche myself up to try and interact with someone. I have learnt to switch it on when I need to.

Unfortunately, though, I soon realise that socialising will not be happening today. I have picked a pandemic to travel in, and there is one man inside and one lady outside, neither of which I have any desire to strike up a conversation with.

Breakfast is dire. If I see any more ham, cheese, and bread, I will scream. It's laid out like a work's canteen, where you slide a tray along a metal rack. None of the food looks good, or at all appetising. It is free, but to be honest, I would rather have paid for a breakfast that I could enjoy. I am probably way too old and fussy to be eating free food in a hostel. I put a few things on my tray and sit down. It's a big food hall and I imagine, in normal times, this would be buzzing with people, but today there are only two of us at far ends of the room. I try the Slovenian plum jam on dry bread – there wasn't any sunflower spread – but it isn't good. The tea is undrinkable. It's in a flask all made up with the milk in already, so it is quite awful. The fruit juice is so watered down that I can't tell what flavour it is.

I grab three hard plums to add to my collection of hard fruit for my room. I am still waiting for my pear from Venice to ripen. I do some laundry and hang it up in my room by the window, which isn't easy. I hang a bra off the cord on the blinds and try to lay out the rest on the windowsill, and pack to go out.

I want to do the walking tour at 11.00 am. It will be my first ever walking tour, but my kids said they are a good way to get to know a place.

I go for a little walk on my own first to see the little bridge with locks on that Ciara and Aidan sent me a photo of last night. I find it and feel quite emotional. It's weird standing on the bridge taking a photo, knowing Ciara, Aidan and Liam stood here doing the same thing four years ago.

I find the big pink building, which isn't difficult as I have already walked past it a few times. I am a little early, and I sit down in a restaurant seating area just by the big pink building, so I can see if people arrive for the walk. I order a watermelon lemonade. It's sharp and delicious, and the sugar will sustain me as I haven't eaten much.

I feel much better today, and I am even considering booking an extra night so that I can explore a bit more. I am booked in tonight, but I think there is more to explore and this trip has been a whirlwind, so I perhaps need to slow down a bit. That might be part of the problem, that I am travelling too fast. I don't fancy travelling again tomorrow, much more than I actually want to stay here for another day. I will see what the walking tour does to me.

There's no point whizzing around Europe. I need to slow it down, not get tired, and enjoy myself. And so what if there is graffiti everywhere, it doesn't need to bother me. Phil says it's your attitude to something that you have the power to change. So, what graffiti? I will ignore the graffiti on the walls and buildings and look at Ljubljana's charm, because it is a charming place.

The walking tour is more a standing tour. Ljubljana centre is very compact and there is a lot of history in this one small space. So, we don't walk very much between the points of interest. I have already seen most of these buildings, but it is good to have the history that comes with them explained.

There is a cute young couple that entertain me on the tour. They aren't a couple when we set off, they have accents but are talking in English. After a little while, I think their conversation has gone wrong but, later, she swings her hair about in front of him again, flirting. There is an obvious attraction. At the end of the tour, he asks her out for a coffee. I wonder if it will develop into anything. They look cute together.

As soon as the tour ends, I'm off to the vegan café, Barbarella. It's along a row of purpose-built shops, which the lady talked about on the tour. A man called Jože Plečnik was responsible for a big proportion of the architecture in Ljubljana, including this building. I passed it yesterday, which is how I know the vegan place is here; I did wonder about it.

It's a very long, narrow building that runs along the side of the river between two bridges. It's a market building full with lots of tiny shops. They are all the same size with a fairly small indoor space for ordering your food, as well as little kitchens and outdoor seats. There are lots of individual eating places and small businesses, all offering different food and produce.

I have a lovely hearty salad bowl with lentils and hummus and a big chunk of what looks like homemade bread. It's very good and exactly what my body needs, some proper nutrition. I eat it slowly and enjoy every single mouthful.

It's the sort of food I wanted to sell in my café. After my divorce, I had a good sum of money from the proceeds of the house, but it wasn't enough to buy my own house, and my credit score was on the floor because of all the debt from the extension and trying to finish the loft conversion. So, even though I had a healthy deposit, I couldn't get a mortgage for the rest. I had to rent a house with the money instead and decided to open a café, a dream of mine.

I did well with the café. It began to show a profit towards the end, but I was fighting a losing battle with it being at the top end of Bodmin High Street. I built up a good menu and had regulars, just not quite enough. I appreciate all those regular faces that came in and ate my food. I don't think they realised how thankful I was that they supported me. My buddha bowl was my bestseller, and I sold hundreds of them during the 15 months I was open.

But what I most wanted to offer was a huge salad bar. Salad is perishable and I just couldn't guarantee it would all be eaten. If I had been in a different town; if I hadn't been distracted with Mint and Marjoram, my frozen food line that I developed while I had my little takeaway shed in St Austell town centre. If even more people had supported the shop, if I hadn't moved house twice in the time that I was open. If, if, if ... then I might have done better and still be open.

Sitting here watching all these people eat this delicious food – which isn't too different from what I was offering – I am a little sad that I didn't make a huge success of my café. I didn't want to fail and, in some ways, I don't think I did. I built it into something unique and sold it on. Doing that was a relief, as it was a nightmare and a dream all rolled into one. There were huge highs when the café was full and buzzing, even guitar-playing sometimes. It was magical. A space that I had created where people came to eat the food I made. Then, such lows when I spent more money on staff than was in the till and the events that I planned just didn't get supported. And the tiredness. I didn't switch off at all in the evenings. I was constantly working on recipes, invoices, social media, a new event, a new dish. New ways to reach more people. And moving house, taking things out of the container to take home after work ... They were tough times and fun times, but the overriding memory is exhaustion; mental and physical like nothing else.

But I had my chance, which is more than most people get. It didn't work and I am OK with that. It took a long while to get over the disappointment, but I did. I now love spending my money in small businesses as I know how very, very difficult it is.

I walk around the market. A small blister that I got in Venice is bothering me a little. I fancy some ripe fruit. Fruit that you can eat today and not have to wait a week to eat. The watermelon looked good from afar, but it is very expensive and as I get closer, I see it is covered in flies. I give it a miss.

As Liam suggested the castle, I think I will do that next. It's begging to be climbed up to, as it's a very dominant feature of Ljubljana. It is a steep climb. I have to stop a few times to catch my breath. The view is worth the climb, though. There are different viewpoints around the base of the castle, so I can see almost 360 degrees. I look down to the streets that I have just walked on and the buildings look pretty and ornate. I take a few selfies and then I walk back down a different way, as there are lots of options.

I find a corner shop and pop in. I really wanted a cold fizzy water but I don't know what 'sparkling' is in Slovenian. So, I get a lemonade, the lady is wrapping watermelon in cling film. It's only 40 cents. That's ridiculously cheap, and it is a good size piece, so I buy some. It was €4.00 on the market. I buy grapes, biscuits, and mushrooms; all for €2.73. I could cook the mushrooms in the kitchen at the hostel just like a proper backpacker.

Back at the hostel, I fall asleep for two hours. That's very unlike me to take a nap, I must have been exhausted. Usually when I try to nap, I only get to that place just above sleep and below being awake, but today I was sound asleep. I even missed some rain, it's wet outside, and I never heard a thing.

I wake up feeling groggy, so I force myself to go back outside or I won't sleep tonight. I book one more night at the reception. The weather looks bad tomorrow and Lake Bled, where I am going next, will be expensive, so I want the best weather I can get. Plus, I am not quite ready to leave. I need to relax a bit more. I am struggling with getting the balance right between chilling, exploring, and travelling. Chilling in a hostel room seems an insane waste of money when you consider how long and how much energy it has taken to get to this part of the world. But whizzing from place to place will make me ill and that's not good either. So, I will do less exploring tomorrow and relax. It feels like the right thing to do. I am not ready for another travel day just yet.

I have a stroll around for an hour and find a proper supermarket. I am in search of sparkling water again. *Pen voda*, I have googled it and written it down this time, but I spot some Strongbow Rosé. What a treat! Every shop I have been in so far is full of beer. So, I buy two of these and some peanut crisp things.

Back in my room, I chill and put some photos on Facebook. A nice little routine at the end of the day, just a handful, so everyone knows I am well and where I have been.

I ring Phil and he tells me he is almost losing the battle with the caterpillars eating the vegetables we are growing. Every time he goes out, there are more and he can't think where they are all hiding. And he has fed Pidgy, our sort of pet pigeon that waits for food. I feel a little homesick.

I am thoroughly enjoying my trip, but Ljubljana has been a bit odd. My expectations were so high that even though I can clearly see its charm now, the whole experience has been ruined a bit by me.

It's the first time on this trip that I have felt a little lonely. This room feels lonely, high up with hardly anyone else here. It's a hostel, and I thought it would be buzzing with people, but I have only seen four other people and none of them even said hello.

I don't have anyone to bounce ideas off or discuss anything with, which for most of the trip has been great because I am free to go wherever I want, whenever I want to. But I don't have anyone to share the good bits with either or tell me not to be so silly.

I have never been a natural people person. Social situations are fraught with anxiety and rules, which makes them stressful. I have a handful of good friends, but I don't collect friends for the sake of it. I have to have a natural connection with people first. I also don't have friends that I ring every day or have a coffee with every couple of days. I keep people slightly at a distance.

I do try not to rely on people and I don't think I am anyone's best friend. I would never be anyone's first phone call if things went wrong. There would always be a closer friend above me. I almost don't want the responsibility. My own life has been so chaotic in the past that I barely have space to sort out what's right in front of me, let alone other people's problems. But if I am called upon, I would do my utter best to help and I hope that I have been a good friend to people.

I have old friends in Essex, where I was born. I went to school with Paula and Sue and catch up on Facebook or with phone calls because of the distance. Elaine is in Essex. I started my nurse training with her at Ipswich hospital in 1989 but unfortunately didn't complete it, which is one of my regrets. Sybil and Sue are in Ipswich, Angela is 'up north,' as well as Sian, one of my oldest friends. All good friends, but so far away. And I have friends in Cornwall – Tami, Cathy, Rachel, Joanne, Tania, Pam, and many more – having lived here for 20 years and raised my children here. I am very blessed.

So, the loneliness is here today, but not something that is going to bother me. I have been on my own now for two weeks, so it's going to affect me a little. And a little bit of loneliness is not a bad thing. The whole point of coming on this trip was to have an adventure and spend some time with myself.

I put such a lot into this trip. Packing in work, leaving Phil for a month, hoping my kids are all OK and don't go and break any bones, or need me to return home at all during this trip.

My brother has gone missing and my mum is now worried about both of us. I should ring her but I have put it off, just sending text messages. I have a bad feeling about his whereabouts. I took my mum with me up to Hangloose to see Aidan in July to give him his birthday present. My mum said that my brother, Stuart, had left the house, but he had not taken any ID with him, no keys, no phone, nothing. There was a moment when I just looked at her and had a sinking feeling. It was a long pause and there was a look on her face. It's a feeling that I have never felt before. Like a mother knows. Who goes out without any ID, or keys? There wasn't anything to say. Of course, I came up with, 'He'll be at a friend's', 'He needs time to himself', etc., etc. But it doesn't feel good and, to be honest, I haven't wanted to ask her if she has heard anything. If it's bad news, she might not tell me so as not to ruin my trip, and if it's good news, she would have rung or texted me. I am scared to ask, which is very selfish.

So, I need to focus. This is a trip of a lifetime. I need to be a bit selfish, even if it feels strange at times. This is a selfish thing to do, leaving Phil at home and taking a long holiday, but I need to enjoy this time as I have created it. I need to treat myself to this adventure, put myself first. I need to think about what happens next and get the absolute best experience that I can out of it.

I go down to get my cider out of the fridge. I open it with great difficulty. I don't have a bottle opener, so I am bashing it against the kitchen work surface, then putting a fork in the top, trying to bend the metal. It takes a while, but I get the lid off and nothing is going to stop me now that I have found some cider. I take it back up to my room and drink it with the last of my hummus and crisps.

And I look for a hotel in Lake Bled. Part of me is excited to go to Bled, but I have to keep that in check, which is a shame in a way because I want to be excited. That's part of this trip, looking forward to the next destination. But I don't want the disappointment.

So, quietly excited, I spend ages researching, making notes. I consider the distance of the bus stop to the hotels that I am looking at. I see a lovely hotel but it looks too far to walk.

The prices are all very different. How much do I want to spend? I don't want to waste money, but I don't want to be tight either. There are two hostels, but they are shared rooms. I don't think I want to do that at Lake Bled. Eventually I decide on a nice hotel with a good breakfast. I hope it's not ham, cheese, and bread again.

My chill evening has been good, I have enjoyed the research. The cider and crisps were delicious and my app says that I walked eight miles today, so a good day.

I am almost asleep until an alarm goes off at 11.30 pm. I ignore it for a bit, thinking someone will turn it off. But it goes on and on, so I open my door and peer up the corridor. I only have my thin short dressing gown on. I can't smell any fire, and no one is rushing around. In fact, it's silent apart from the alarm. I go back to bed, but it's very difficult to switch off. The noise continues and I get up again and peep out of the door and listen for people. Perhaps they all left and I am the only one here. I look out of the window, no fire engines or flashing lights. I go back to bed but I can't sleep till I know what's going on, so I get dressed and put my passport in my bag, the only vital thing I need and open the door.

A girl is going into her room on the other side of the staircase. I have not seen her before and I don't know her nationality. She doesn't look stressed, and I need to say something before she disappears into her room. So, I ask her if she knows what the noise is. She says she doesn't know. I say, 'No fire then', and she says all is OK. So, I go back to bed, and eventually the noise goes off and I sleep like a log.

Wednesday 12th August

I have a lie in because the breakfast is not worth getting out of bed for. I drink a fruit juice that I bought at Lake Como in the supermarket and eat my last ripe plum from Venice and a fruit pot from Cornwall. I must stop carrying food around as there are supermarkets everywhere. I'm not in the jungle, and I don't need to carry supplies.

I go down and collect my watermelon and grapes from the fridge and fill up my water bottle. I need to go to the bus station to book a bus ticket to Bled for 11.00 am tomorrow and then I will go to Tivoli Park.

It's a big park and I walk around for a bit and find a bench with a view of the castle and skyscraper that the walking tour lady pointed out yesterday. Well, it was obvious to see as it's very tall, but I didn't know the public could go in it. The bench is a great spot, looking over a lovely green lawn and a selection of trees. It's still and quiet and I feel my body breathe out.

This is a beautiful spot. I eat my watermelon and some grapes and look at the castle in the distance that I went up to yesterday.

I was going to walk around the park for a few hours, but I am quite happy sitting on the bench with this lovely view. I can't read any of the park signposts anyway, so I am going to stop *doing*, and just *be*.

I have read a lot of books on meditating, spirituality, and being in the moment. I have been on two retreats to Sharpham House in Devon, which I loved. It's a very special place. I was nervous going in the first time, wondering if it was all a bit hippy-dippy and weird, but it was amazing and I didn't want to leave. It's a big stone house, set on a hill overlooking the River Dart. A beautiful location, with lovely grounds and a walled vegetable garden. The house has the most amazing, unique oval staircase that I used to walk up and down just for the fun of it. Sharpham House is magical, stunning, relaxing, and humble all at the same time.

I have done a lot of 'doing' on this trip, whizzing around towns and cities collecting miles on my app, and I haven't done much 'being' on this trip. I want to explore all the places that I go to or why would I go to them? So that means I have been very busy. But this is my second whole day in Ljubljana and I did a lot yesterday, so there's not much left to explore today. Hopefully, I will stop whizzing about and slow down.

My friends on Facebook have been saying they are jealous of my travels. Maybe jealous is too strong a word, envious perhaps.

As I sit here in the lovely park and look at the expanse of green in front of me and beautiful tree-lined paths with memories of Venice, of the Panoramic express in Switzerland, Morzine and Lake Geneva, I can see what they mean. But who would honestly be jealous of me? I've had some difficult times that I wouldn't wish on anyone. I am only here now, possibly because my life fell apart, and I had to pick all the pieces up and find a new way.

I had to sell the family home after my divorce and Ciara turning 18 and I didn't want to. The kids were settled and we would all have just rather stayed there as it was our home. When Liam came home from Brighton and Ciara from university in London, it was their base. Aidan and Jamie's had good-sized rooms with all their things around them. We were close to town, so they could go out of an evening and not worry about buses. The gym was over the road and train station was a five minutes' walk away.

I could afford the mortgage. I had been paying it for a couple of years on my own, but I couldn't put it in my name because I didn't earn enough.

Such a ridiculous situation to be in, because after having to sell up and leave, I had to rent a house that cost twice as much as the mortgage. A classic case of the world has gone crazy. And the rented houses were not ours. We couldn't hang anything on the walls, it just wasn't home. It made me so cross that I had been forced into this situation.

I had to manage the kids' disappointment at leaving a house they were familiar with to live in a pokey rented house in Roche. I had the third room and I have seen bigger cupboards. I had a mattress on the floor that I got in the charity shop. And Liam and Ciara had no home to come home to, nothing familiar and it broke my heart and was so tough. Then we had to move after six months because it was a winter rental. We only stayed in the next house in Luxulyan for seven months as we all wanted to get back to St Austell. When Ciara came home once from university, she was trapped in the village and in a house she didn't know and all her things were in boxes. The buses in and out of the village were very sketchy.

But on a positive note, I now live with Phil. Jamie seems OK where he is. Aidan and his girlfriend, Thea have a lovely little rented flat, which they can just about afford and I don't have any property at all. Scary but freeing as well. So, my finances are back in order again.

Maybe my friends wish they could go on a trip like this. I can't believe it's money stopping them as most of my friends own their own houses or have very small mortgages. They could release some money to do this. Some of them still have responsibilities toward their children and that would stop you from travelling. My children are all independent now and the money I am using is inherited from my Uncle Bob.

So, I feel free enough to do this. Phil hasn't stood in my way either, other people's partners might not be as happy with the idea. Phil wasn't ecstatic about me travelling alone, but he knew I wanted to do it and we can travel together next year.

This is such a nice spot and a good idea to stop and rest. I can feel myself unwinding which is really needed.

After a couple of hours of sitting on the bench, I leave the park feeling a little lighter. Some time with myself unravelling my life has helped. I have so much to be thankful for. I think consciously slowing down has helped me and those couple of hours sat on that bench was well spent. It's almost lunch, so I head back to the vegan café.

Today I order a protein bowl with black beans, chickpeas and warm quinoa. It is all cooked to perfection with a lovely dressing. I am also having a cheeky glass of Slovenian wine at €1.30. Why not? It's the middle of the day, but I am chilling. I'm on holiday and I feel content. This trip to Ljubljana has been a pivotal point in my trip. I have to learn to slow down on this trip ... and also in life.

My protein bowl is delicious. I eat it slowly, like they taught me at Sharpham House and taste every mouthful, feeling it nourishing me. It's very filling and takes ages to eat, but I am in no hurry. I am watching the world go by in this busy little spot. I honestly feel different since sitting on that park bench.

Afterwards I go for a stroll around the market but it's the same as yesterday. I need some new clothes and was hoping to find a stall I liked.

So, I go for a casual walk by the river and find a street that I haven't been to before. I find a dress shop and buy a useful dress that is only €10. There are so many sales on it is a bit sad, COVID-19 has damaged all the businesses all over the world. The boats that go up and down the river are, at best, half full. One boat had only two people on it yesterday and they must take 50 people at the height of the season.

It's not a dress I would probably have bought at home, but I like it all the same. It's comfortable, easy to wear, and doesn't need ironing. Also, it will be a new dress to wear in the hotel tomorrow. It's an expensive hotel at just over €100 a night. But it's a treat and it will be nice to have a new dress to wear and not look like a backpacker. I leave the shop, swinging the posh branded paper bag, a rarity for me. I buy most of my clothes at charity shops or The Bridge Agency in St Austell.

I decide to go for a drink at the top of the skyscraper. It is the one thing left that I really want to do in Ljubljana.

It turns out to be a huge palaver trying to get to the top. None of the three lifts will work. A lady leaves because of it, but I want to get to the top and I am quite capable of climbing a few stairs. Maybe I could pick the lift up on floor two or three. But no, I walk up to the tenth floor, round and round the spiral staircase, all the way to the top, and almost collapse in a heap from heat and exertion.

The door is locked. Hmmm. There's a note on the door that says to go back down to floor nine and go up to floor 10 by the lift. The lift won't stop at 10, so I go to 11. I get out and spot some toilets; great. So I pop in and when I come out, I see a barrier across a set of stairs that goes up one more flight to the restaurant. I can see the restaurant, and the sky, but not how to get to it. The instructions on the barrier say to take the lift to floor 12. So that's what I do.

Oh my, what a view. It was worth all that fuss. A whole 360 degrees on four sides, with a single layer of tables next to a glass barrier, all the way around. It isn't very big, maybe five tables on each side, and it is quiet. I think I know why. In fact, I am surprised anyone made it here at all.

I walk all the way around, taking photos. I can see the exact bench that I was sitting on this morning, eating my melon. It looks tiny from up here. I can see the castle and the buildings with their terracotta roof tiles. On one side, I count four churches and each one has a clock, all different in size and character. The buildings are so tall, you can't see the river, you wouldn't know there was a river at all from up here.

I take a few photos and sit down next to the railings. A lady takes my order for a cup of tea and a slice of traditional Slovenian cake. I am not expecting to drink the tea, but I can't sit here with nothing in front of me and I fancy a slice of traditional Slovenian cake. I have no idea what to expect from the catering, but I love the view.

The tea turns out to be the best that I have had on my travels in Europe, except at Liam's house. They even have oat milk.

The weather is perfect, there's supposed to be a 70% chance of rain but I don't think it's arriving. I could have gone to Bled, but this has been a real treat and I feel I have seen all there is to see in Ljubljana and having a slower day has been good for me.

I need to think about what to do after Lake Bled. What do I still want to get out of this trip? Saturday will be halfway through if I do a whole month. It makes sense to do a whole month and as much as I want a hug from Phil and one of his jacket potatoes, I have invested money, time and emotion in this trip and I need to get the next bit right.

I can't go to Serbia, Montenegro, or Mostar as in my original plan because of COVID-19 restrictions. I might go to Zagreb, Slovakia, Hungary and Germany. Maybe three days in each so I can unwind. I also don't want to go to a country just for the sake of it. So I might not go to Slovakia, I might spend four days in Budapest and stop in Germany. Liam recommended Heidelberg. There's lots to think about.

This is a perfect way to spend an afternoon. There is so much to look at right off into the distance as well as close up. It feels fresh and clear up here. Surrounded by blue sky, my mind feels clearer, and I feel calmer for it. Ljubljana has been a mix of highs and lows, managing my expectations. This interlude at the top of the skyscraper is another highlight of my trip.

Perhaps not everyone wants to do a trip like this. A lot of people like their two weeks in Spain or Greece or the UK. I like to do that too. But this feels like an adventure and not everyone wants an adventure. It's been great for my geography of Europe, learning and studying the map every night, working out where to go next. It's not relaxing like a week in Spain. I keep changing counties, currency, trains. I am always looking for new places to sleep and eat and things to do. But it has been so much fun, and probably easier and much richer than I ever thought it would be.

I order another cup of tea as it's so good and I am enjoying it up here. But after a long wait, the young lad says the coffee machine has broken and he hasn't any hot water. That's a shame and frustrating, as so far I haven't wanted a second cup of tea anywhere.

I eventually leave to go back to my room. I accidentally buy another dress on the way home, now I will throw a top away. I brought clothes with me to throw away, old ones on their last legs that were going to be recycled, knowing it would make room for the odd treat if I saw it.

I post on Facebook, pack my bag and go to sleep.

Leaving Ljubljana
Thursday 13th August

I didn't get off to sleep till gone one and then I had some bad dreams.

It's the PTSD. I was only diagnosed a couple of years ago and, to be honest, it was a relief. It's something I can now work with, try to understand, and hopefully heal from.

Everything we go through in life has an impact on us and we all seem to go through something different. Not one of us has the same story to tell, but every experience that we have will affect us.

Being in an abusive marriage for 20 years has affected me. It wasn't always bad. I would be a complete liar to say that it was. Sometimes it was good and sometimes it was neutral, but the alcohol often made my ex-husband bad-tempered and often aggressive. Walking on eggshells, waiting for something to happen is not a healthy way to live.

When you are in danger, you use your flight or fight response, you either leave the situation to make yourself safe or fight to protect yourself. When you are in a domestic situation, it's often just not possible to get away safely, especially if you have to collect up a couple of kids on the way out. The time spent doing that would put you in more danger, and you can't fight, not against a drunk man. Instead, your body freezes to protect you.

Thankfully, the bad dreams are getting fewer and fewer. They were very intense shortly after my marriage ended as I tried to process everything that had happened to me and make some sense of it all. Now they pop up suddenly, without any warning. Maybe because I had a chill day yesterday, my brain was more relaxed. I don't know; I don't understand it, I just live with it.

So I am not feeling as refreshed today as I'd hoped, but it's OK. I am almost packed and only have to walk to the bus station and then sit on a bus for an hour and a half. It's not a major travel day and I am excited. Yes, I am allowing myself to be excited. I am going to Lake Bled, and it looks beautiful in the photos.

I can't wait to get there and check into a nice hotel with maybe a decent breakfast. It looks like it had nice views of the lake and I think it has a pool. A posh hotel, I can't wait.

I will pop to breakfast and see if it's improved, or maybe take some fruit, or make a cup of green tea in the hostel kitchen and then get on my way.

At 10.15 am, I am sitting in the 'terminal lounge' a cafe with an indoor/outdoor seating area at the bus and train station in Ljubljana. I have three-quarters of an hour, so perfect timing for a cup of tea, and chill on the cushy chairs. It's already very warm.

There's catchy music playing, some 70s boogie-woogie stuff which is right up my street, and so English, which is very strange at a bus stop in Slovenia. The waitress is a bit confused by my request for tea, which seems odd as it's on the drinks' menu. I will see what turns up. I don't really want a drink, but I do want to sit here in the comfy chairs and buying a drink is what you are supposed to do.

I have been thinking of going to Graz, in Austria. I don't have a set plan after Lake Bled and I have studied the map and asked for advice on the Interrail page. The man in the ticket office here couldn't have been more helpful. He says from Ljubljana to Maribor was OK, but Maribor to Graz is five hours as it goes around the long way. There are probably mountains in the way. He gives me a map and a printed timetable, so I feel more confident and I might book a hotel in Graz.

It's been a big decision not to go to Croatia and Plitvice Lakes. I would love to but the reality is there are too many buses and transfers and I would have to double back on myself as I can't continue to Serbia and Mostar because of the pandemic. And Austria looks nice.

I am on the bus to Lake Bled now. I have done some research and there are three bus stops, so when I got on I told the driver the name of my hotel and asked him which is the best bus stop to get off at. He said it's the third stop and assured me he will tell me when to get off. The little town of Bled looks good and we pause at the bus station. There are lots of eating places and a road leading down to the lake. It looks lovely, small but touristy, and a nice number of people are wandering about.

We drive along the edge of the lake and I am getting ready to get off, it must be here. I fleetingly look at the lake, which is beautiful, but I am now concentrating on looking for my hotel. The driver stops and signals it's my stop.

I get off and look around. We are at the far end of the lake. I thought I had booked one a bit closer to the centre, not that's there's a centre by the looks of it, but the other end is definitely busier.

I get my phone out, switch my data on and get Google Maps out. It's 17 minutes' walk away. He's dropped me in the wrong place, what a horrible man. I know 17 minutes is not far usually, but when it's about 30°C and you have a month's belongings on your back, it's not funny.

I sweat all the way back along the edge of the lake, the way the bus drove. It's so hot today and my bag is heavy. I find my hotel and it doesn't look right, it's not at all how I pictured it. It's very close to the main busy road which wasn't obvious from the photos. It's close to the lake, but the big hotel in front of it is much closer and I just can't see how there's going to be a view of the lake. It's 1.30 pm and I am a bit early for check-in but it's worth a try. The front door is through the carpark, which again wasn't in the photos. It doesn't have much land, and it doesn't feel like the little bit of luxury I wanted. It's OK inside, it feels like a hotel which is nice after the hostel. But it's not quite what I pictured. Although, I am a bit excited. I picture a cute bedroom, a toilet in my room instead of across a hall, plush towels, and a little luxury.

The man at reception can't find my booking. He takes my passport and says that I am not on the system. Oh, dear. Then, oh yes, he can see it, the booking is for next Thursday. This cost me over €200 and I can't be here in Lake Bled next Thursday. What a mess.

He is very helpful, considering it is entirely my own fault. He makes phone calls to his colleagues, looking for a room while I scan Booking.com. Thank goodness I have data.

There are about 23 other places I could stay tonight, so after looking around at the hotel, I think maybe it's been a blessing. I can't see a view and it's not as spacious as I was hoping.

It's a right pain in the butt, as I wanted to just plonk my stuff down and get out and enjoy the lake and the sunshine. I wasn't expecting to try and find somewhere to sleep and this was going to be a treat after three nights in a hostel. But this hotel would just have been a waste of money.

He is very sorry he has been on the phone for a good ten minutes, by which time I have managed to cancel the booking for next week as it's so far in the future and easy to cancel. I just press a few buttons on my phone and I haven't I lost any money. I thank him very much and get out of there before he finds a room, as I really don't want it now.

Now what? I find a bench down by the lake, but even that ten-minute walk is hard work. The lake is stunning, but I can't enjoy it just yet, not until I can get this bag off my back.

A lot of hotels are €90 for one night. There's a cheap hostel, and it has very good reviews but it's sharing a dorm, which I don't want to do. There are a few guesthouses, but I am getting confused and they are all blending into one. I don't like the look of any one in particular and I can't make a decision. The sensible thing is to just go to the hostel, it's 10 minutes away.

I get almost get there and stop. I just can't do it. I can't bear the thought of sharing a dorm, even if the reviews are good. I sit on another bench. I google a hotel that I can see from the bench. It looks amazing right on the edge of the lake. But it's very expensive. It isn't even in my expensive-treat-yourself price range. Shame as it looks lovely, right on the lake and luxurious, but I can't justify the price.

I google a couple of guesthouses and I can't make a decision. I am hungry and not thinking straight. Right, I pick one, put it in Google. It's €50 a night, and it's 15 minutes away. Off I go. It's behind the first hotel up into a residential area. I go to the wrong place and a man says it's over the road, not far. I go in as the front door is open. It has a large reception area for what looks like a house, and I take a seat on the chair at the bottom of the wooden stairs. I look at my phone and something doesn't feel right. I have put the wrong postcode in the satnav. This is not the €50 a night place, it's €90 a night. For beep's sake. I will just pay the €90... that's €180 to stay here, or have only one night here and move again. I don't want to pack and move again tomorrow. I want two nights in the same place.

I make a snap decision and leave quickly before anyone sees me. What a nightmare.

I put the correct postcode in and you won't believe it, but it's just by the hostel, back over the other side, near the bench that I was sitting on. I am struggling to keep upbeat now. I am running very low on energy and enthusiasm. The bag is so heavy now that it actually hurts. Sweat is dripping down my back. I am tired, annoyed with myself, and cross that I am wasting time. By now, I should be wandering around the lake, bag-free.

I get on with it, just put one foot in front of the other. I don't have any other choice. I haven't booked either and can't be bothered to stop and book it on Booking.com. I hope that no one turns up in the next 20 minutes. It's a gamble.

It's in a residential area but the house looks cute and full of character. Bajtica Guesthouse. There is a seating area with soft chairs and a low table and cushions outside under a canopy. It looks lovely and I want to instantly re-create this seating area in our garden in Cornwall.

The front door is hard to find. It's around the back and it all looks a bit cluttered. I have second thoughts. But I see the Tripadvisor sticker on the window: 9.3 which is a fantastic score. I knock and a surprised lady answers, as she's not expecting anyone. I have no idea what to say to her. I rattle off garbage about hotels and overbooking, and here I am. I must look a sight. She takes me over to the seating area and asks if I would like a lemonade while she gets the room ready. I can stay. I am happy and yes, please, lemonade would be perfect. The lady brings back lemonade with fresh mint in it. She is kind and lovely and helpful. She brings out a map and explains the area to me. There is a gorge that I didn't know about and a map of the lake. I study it while she goes to make the bed. I feel a bit bad putting her on the spot, but she is coping well and with not a sign of annoyance at all.

She shows me to my room. It's a family home, full of treasures and knick-knacks and dark wood. The room is perfect and it looks vaguely familiar from the google searches but it's better in real life. And there's a shared bathroom, big and clean and very modern. She suggests I have a shower. Oh dear, that's the second time on this trip.

After my shower, I change and decide to go to the gorge. I will do that today as it's a half-day here now and I will spend all day at the lake tomorrow. My landlady suggests getting a bus as it's 45 minutes on foot. But I think after the day I have had a gentle, backpack-free walk will be lovely and help me unwind. I am a bit tense and stressed.

In my urgency to get out and enjoy my time here and the sunshine, I forget to refill my water bottle. The heat is intense and I only have fruit in my belly. It's a struggle and not the leisurely walk I was hoping for. There are not many signposts and I am just following paths and hoping for the best, which is not relaxing. I probably should have got the bus, or just chilled at the lake and done this tomorrow. Less haste, more speed, is what I needed today.

It's a long walk, probably an hour, and it's not very relaxing. Why did I just run out of the house with minimal preparation and assumed that I would find my way to a gorge in the middle of Slovenia? I am so annoyed with myself. If I just slowed down a bit, I would get on faster. This isn't a race. This is what I do all the time, here and at home. I feel like I have to squeeze in as much as I can. I should have found a bar near the lake and had some food and a drink, not hike on roads across the Slovenian landscape. I am too worried about whether I am going in the right direction to enjoy the scenery.

I pass a really lovely stream and I can feel that it's going to be pretty. The water in the stream is clear with hints of green. I am here, thank goodness for that.

The gorge is €10. I wasn't expecting that and I have to buy water and that's €2.50 and it's only tiny. One gulp and it will be gone which is daylight robbery.

But it's so worth it, the gorge is phenomenal. One of nature's gifts. There is a wooden walkway crossing back and forth across the river so you can stop and take amazing photos, and the sides of the gorge are tall and rocky. The water is so bright and clear; the river is running fast and noisily over rocks into mini waterfalls. The colours are amazing, blues, greens, turquoise. It's truly lovely, and then it's over and I find myself at the end. I want to go back and do it again, but I went through the barrier and out into nowhere. I should have done that slower as well. What's the hurry? What am I trying to achieve?

The signage at the end is rubbish but clearly says that the quickest way back to Bled is through the trees, and I remember the landlady talking about a nice cool walk through the pine trees. There isn't another way unless you have paid the €10 to go back. I start to walk through the trees, climb up and walk over gnarly tree roots on a sort of path, but there are no signposts.

The track I am following seems to get narrower and doesn't feel well worn. I put my data on and look at Google Maps. It says I am not on the red line, but I can't get to it. It doesn't seem to exist. This is the only visible path of sorts. I go back to the beginning and see a family walk down from the woods. Maybe this is it.

I follow the route the family came down, walking over the exposed trees roots. It still doesn't seem right, and it feels like it is getting dark. My phone's battery is low from using it so much today, trying to find accommodation and directions. And of course, in the hurry to get out of the guesthouse and enjoy the rest of the day, I have forgotten my power-pack. So the day I might actually need it, I don't have it with me. I have another quick look, but it still says that I am not on the right path.

I am genuinely scared, and I feel so unsafe. Apart from the family, there is no one around. The pine trees are dense and it is quite dark in the woods and there are no signposts. It's getting late and I could very easily get lost. I get lost on the main roads so I don't stand a chance in here.

I continue. It's cool and the pine trees look like soldiers, lined up so neatly in rows as far into the woods as I can see. All I want to do is get through it and see some daylight and feel safe. Some of the paths are uphill, so I am out of breath and worn out.

Today has been a very strange day.

There's absolutely no one around. What if a strange man tries to attack me? I wouldn't stand a chance. I did order a personal alarm, but arrived a week after. That would have made me feel a bit better.

How much further? What if I'm going the wrong way? I want this to be over, so I walk faster, half jogging but also trying to reserve some energy in case a man does chase me. What a ridiculous situation to get myself into.

At last, daylight ahead. I slow down considerably now. I am safe and I walk out of the woods into the daylight. I am so happy that I feel a bit emotional.

Everyone at home would be annoyed with me for being so unprepared and putting myself in danger, but I honestly couldn't see another way. And I am here, out of the woods, back into the sunshine and daylight.

I walk along the path, looking at the views. There are huge mountains in the distance and the little village of Zasip in front of me, which is so pretty. The views across the landscape are breath-taking. I stop. I tell myself not to move another step. Stop rushing, it's a lesson that I keep telling myself, but then ignore.

So I stop. Physically stop moving and take a moment at the side of the road to take it all in and take a photo. I must slow this whole trip right down. I've hardly noticed any of this beautiful landscape while I have been walking here. I was concentrating on the roads and worrying about the time.

The land is very flat and Bled is difficult to see, as there are clusters of pine trees in front of it. The huge, gently sloping mountains to the left against the flatness is breath-taking. There is a pretty little white church with a terracotta roof just in front of me and lush, green grass. The sun is weaker now and casting shadows across the mountains, with a hint of pink in the sky. I take a deep lungful of fresh, Slovenian air and remind myself how privileged I am to be here in this beautiful place. I walk back to Bled much slower, picking up the road that got me here.

I head straight to the vegan place that I googled on the bus to get something to eat. I am absolutely famished. It is tucked inside an outdoor shopping precinct and isn't easy to find.

The burger is amazing, huge, and difficult to eat as the generous filling keeps sliding out the bun. It is truly delicious and very satisfying. I even have a glass of wine with it. Cider is impossible to find and I like a glass of wine occasionally. Actually, I love wine, but it makes me drunk very quickly and gives me an enormous headache, so I drink it in moderation now.

It is 8.30 pm by the time I have finished and I head back to the guesthouse.

I shower again and clean my teeth. The landlady is on the landing halfway up the stairs with a bottle of red wine in her hands. Would I like a glass with her? That's so sweet, but I don't like red wine, I have my dressing gown on, I am shattered and I just want to chill. I thank her, it's very hospitable of her. She asks if I would like tea in the morning and what type. I like this lady. I don't know if breakfast is included, as I didn't even know I was going to be here. I guess not, but that's OK, tea will be great. I say I will be up around nine. She says she is home all day, so not to worry.

I love my room; the window faces the mountains and it looks lovely as night draws in. I watch the sky change colours. It reminds me of a lovely lady that I met at Sharpham House, who had us all lying on the floor at the bottom of the oval staircase staring up at the sky through the roof light, watching the sky go through all the shades of blue, from indigo to midnight blue. That was a very special moment in time and so is this.

I go on Facebook and put some photos up, downplaying my day so people don't worry. I don't mention the walk through the woods on my own. My app says that I walked over seven miles.

I message Phil and tell him how lovely it is here. Then I go to sleep, it's been quite a day and I am glad it ended well.

Lake Bled

Friday 14th August

Oops.

I go down at about 10 am. I was exhausted and overslept. I take my little pot of green tea with me, in case my landlady doesn't have tea that I like. I go into the kitchen and the man and lady from Munich that are staying in the room next to me are in the garden, eating breakfast. There is a window in the kitchen with shutters, which are open so I can see the front garden. There is a table underneath the window outside, a bit lower than the kitchen where the Germans are sitting. The table in the kitchen is all laid out with pots of jam and plates. The landlady has gone to the bookstore. I didn't realise breakfast was included; I misunderstood. I could have set an alarm and come down at nine.

I boil the kettle to make some green tea. I never let politeness get in the way of a cup of tea, so I just help myself to the kettle. Then I go out into the covered area that I sat in yesterday. It feels wrong sitting at the kitchen table and I like a cup of green tea first to wake my body up. It's lovely to sit outside and wake up slowly. Plus, I adore this little seated area. I want one.

The lady returns on her bike and says, 'Come, come,' and gestures for me to follow her. She explains that she's had breakfast. I feel bad, she was going to eat with me but when I explain I had a much-needed lie-in she says not to apologise, it's all good.

She makes me an omelette without asking. This vegan thing is not going well. I don't have the heart to refuse it, and it does look good. I haven't had an omelette in about five or six years. She pours me tea from the pot she made before she went to the bookshop. It's tepid and I like my tea to scald me but I drink it anyway as she has been so kind. So I have two cups of tea now: tepid, black Earl Grey, and my hot green tea. My landlady is lovely. She tells me a story about her uncle and Earl Grey tea. When he was in England, he sent it home to her as a child and she shows me her cupboard full of different teas.

The omelette is delicious. She has added chives, herbs, and rocket from the garden.

She cuts me some cheese that's on the table and explains its origins. It's made in the mountains by someone she knows who only sells it to locals, so it's not available in the shops. The cows are fed the lush grass on the mountains. I have already had the omelette and cheese in Venice on my pizza so I just try some. Why not? I won't get the chance ever again. I don't eat much because it's precious and not cheap and it's very good. She refills my not-so-hot tea, it's not so bad. At least it tastes like quality tea. Then I have bread, no butter, and some of her homemade raspberry jam and apricot jam, both of which are delicious. She can certainly make jam.

She has made such an effort and is lovely and I like her a lot. We chat very easily.

I tell her about my trip to the gorge and getting lost in the woods and my concerns. She says that I was perfectly safe. Bled is a very safe place and that nothing would ever have happened. I can't imagine living anywhere where that's true.

I return to my room, my belly full and happy, and hang up the laundry that I washed in the shower out of the window. Probably not the look the landlady was going for, but I need it to dry today.

I am going to walk around the lake at last. There were lots of people swimming when I drove by on the bus and walked back on foot. There was a very shallow bit where the bus driver dropped me off. So I put my swimming costume on under my clothes. There is only a 1% chance of me actually going in, but you never know, and if it feels right, I might. Plus, all my underwear is hanging out of the window, wet. So it's probably best that I wear something.

On the way out, my landlady suggests I get a cup of tea at a hotel called Villa Bled, where there is a café called Belvedere Café.

Off I go for a leisurely stroll around Lake Bled. After 10 minutes, I think I have gone the wrong way. After 20 minutes, I see a 'You are leaving Bled' sign, which confirms it. Stupid girl. I find my way back to the lake. Goodness knows what I did wrong but I am on the lake now and I just need to follow it.

The hotel has a huge, wide staircase leading up to it. I would not normally have walked up to it unless I was staying here, which is highly unlikely, as it looks very expensive. I find a seating area with a view of the lake and the island in the middle of it. It is stunning. I ask the waiter for the drinks menu. He kindly points to the café sign and sends me politely up to the café. I think I might have been in the residents' only section. He assures me the view is even better from the café.

He is right, it's breath-taking. Thank you, Mrs Landlady, for this amazing piece of local knowledge. I don't think I would have got that level of care at the hotel I nearly stayed at. There is a single row of seats next to the viewing area and I order tea and fizzy water. I then breathe out and just sit and look at the tranquil picture postcard scene in front of me.

It's a piece of heaven. The tea is harsh and bitter, and the water only half fizzy, which is worse than being still but nothing is going to ruin this moment in time with this amazing view in front of me, it's perfect. Being so high up, it's peaceful and quiet and there are hardly any other customers. I can occasionally hear laughter from the edge of the water where people are swimming.

The island in the centre of the lake looks so pretty with its white church and terracotta roof and the water in the lake is a stunning blue, almost turquoise in places, and the whole scene is framed by mountains. When I was walking here, the water was so clear that I could see the ducks' legs moving. But from up here, the water is very blue. I can hear the oars of a boat going out to the island, and see paddleboards making their way out, leaving ripples on the water. It isn't a big island, but it has a church and building on it and a very steep, wide set of stairs leading up to the church.

I could get on a boat and go on the lake or over to the island, but I don't feel the need.

I could sit here all day, but eventually, after an hour or so, I tear myself away. The waitress takes a full length photo of me which makes a change.

I walk to where the horrible bus driver dropped me yesterday. It's a fair walk without a backpack on and I laugh to myself.

There are lots of people swimming and the 1% of me is very tempted. There's a gentle incline, so it looks safe. I am not a strong swimmer, but I am seriously tempted. Phil would be in by now, or any of my kids, without a second thought. I wish I could just not think and get in as I know I would enjoy it. But where would I put my bag? I am on my own, it might get pinched while I was swimming and even if it didn't, I would be looking at it the whole time. I am such a worrier.

I also prefer to have someone with me when I am swimming. I got into trouble at Grange-over-Sands when I was about 10 years old and had to swim for my life. Me and my brother, Stuart, had walked out to a sort of bank of sand and the water hadn't gone above our knees. We walked along, parallel with the beach, waving at our mum and younger sister, Susan, who were walking with us but on the beach, separated by the water. Then we decided to go back to the beach. We walked back into the water, but it got deeper and deeper and we fell off a ledge and couldn't touch the bottom. We had to swim or drown. We both did doggy paddle all the way back to shore. I have never been very comfortable in open water since. I watch the people enjoying the water for a bit, envious of them.

I continue walking round the lake and get to a much busier bit. There's a café and lots of people swimming, lots of families, people sunbathing, the smell of pizza in the air.

As I walk further on near the castle, there is a controlled swimming area which is heaven if you are a child. It has a spiral slide and barriers in the water to stop anyone drifting out into the lake. It looks so much fun. I stop and watch for a bit. I see a little boy of about five in the queue for the spiral slide, and he is naked. He goes down on his tummy and I pray there are no sharp seams in the plastic or he will be in trouble. I move on. I can't bear to watch.

It starts to drizzle; it didn't look like it was going to rain. I was in complete sunshine up at the café. I must have a rain fairy with me. I go back to the guesthouse and sit outside at the table under the kitchen window where the Munich people had breakfast. It has a shelter over it so while it's raining so I can be outside and still stay dry. I do like this house. The landlady's daughter makes me a pot of tea with my green tea in a small silver teapot on a tray and I feel quite special sitting there at the table.

Phil would love it here.

By 4.30 pm the rain has eased and I am really hungry again. It's time to go back to the vegan place that I was at yesterday. Public Bar and Vegan Kitchen Bled. I walk back over to the lake. I am not eating here again because I am feeling bad about the omelette or the Heidi-inspired mountain cheese, but because it was delicious yesterday, and I had planned to come back and have the potato pie. I have no idea what it is. The lady yesterday mentioned lentils, so it could go either way. But the food yesterday was so good, I am feeling hopeful.

I research buses to Zagreb while I wait for my meal. Graz, in Austria, is going to take me all day with a two-and-a-half-hour break at Maribor. That's OK with no backpack on, but Trieste was hard work for an hour and a half and very frustrating, not being able to explore.

So, I decide on Zagreb with no idea what's happening after that. It's more a geography option. It's a big place and I should be able to get to anywhere easily from there once I have decided. Maybe Budapest. I am not sure.

The food is amazing. I have never eaten anything like it and would love the recipe. So many flavours packed into a very generous triangle portion of the pie and it's nesting on a big base of salad and coleslaw. It's absolutely delicious.

I book a hostel with a private room in Zagreb which is €60 for two nights. I don't especially want to go to Zagreb. There's nothing there I particularly want to do, but who knows? It might be amazing and I don't know where else to go.

As I leave the restaurant, it starts to rain. I brought a funky plastic Poundland coat thing, which would be useful right now, but it's in my room. I don't have a coat as I accidentally left that in Morzine, hanging on Liam's coat rack, because I used it that first overcast day. So, I am going to get wet. It's only six o'clock and I don't want to go back yet. I look for somewhere to get a drink, but all the outside seating is wet and I don't want to be inside. The vegan café is tucked in the corner of the shopping precinct and I didn't go for the view, as there wasn't one, just the food.

I find somewhere dry with a view of the lake, and the castle. It's perfect. I order wine again, as there is no cider on the menu. It's very dark, with thunder clouds overhead and quite chilly. I don't have a cardigan, but it's still lovely. I didn't go up to the castle, I ran out of time. I perhaps should have stayed in Bled for three nights, but originally, I was booked into an expensive hotel and two nights was plenty of money and I know the guesthouse is full tomorrow. So that's not an option. If I book another guesthouse, I will have a few hours during the day with my backpack and I don't want that. Apart from the castle, I think I have done everything, but a chill day here would have been lovely.

I drink my wine, it's very nice, and the waitress brings me a little saucer of peanuts, but I am quite full from dinner. Anyway, it's getting very cold and the rain isn't easing at all, so I just need to make a run for it. I think I know the way now: follow the path around the lake, turn right, then left at a hotel, and follow the road up to the ambulance station. I put my phone, camera, and power pack in the middle of my bag so they don't get wet and put my sun hat on for protection and make a dash.

I have a shower and ring Phil. He reminds me that during this trip I was going to send three words from the app to tell him where I am exactly. So, that's what I do. He can immediately see where I am, and he says he thought I would be up the other end of the lake.

He is pleased to see where I am.

I post a few photos on Facebook and then I get my Kindle out for the first time on the trip. I had brought two real books but left them at Liam's. I continue reading a book that I forgot I had already started back home. I chill in my lovely room with the amazing view of the mountains.

Bled to Zagreb
Saturday 15th August

Today is Assumption Day. I learn that at breakfast. To celebrate the day, my landlady has organised a literary event with Slovenian stories in a boat on the lake. But of course, there is thunder and lightning and it's raining heavily so the event has been cancelled. She says the 15th August is often bad weather. Her friends met here at the house last night and drank wine and laughed instead, she apologises for the noise. I did hear a few people, but it wasn't loud at all. So today, I got up before her and met her on the landing. She probably wanted a lie in today. We aren't really in sync in the mornings.

I have another delicious non-vegan breakfast. She's been into the garden to get an even bigger handful of herbs and rocket.

Her English is fluent, and she says that there's no point getting emotional when things go wrong and that insight comes with age. A lot of work had gone into preparing the celebrations, but it wasn't to be. She makes a lot of sense. It's raining, and even though she had put a lot of effort in and it hasn't gone ahead, she isn't going to let it get to her. She says there's no point spending another minute being upset by it.

She tells me some of the histories of Slovenia, and Italians and Venetians along the coast to Croatia. About an island where everyone got on a boat overnight and disappeared. And how her family left Slovenia one by one in the 1940s because of the political situation and she was the first from her family to return in the 70s. It is a true delight having met her and a highlight on my trip so far.

I go to my room and pack. I decide that the PG Tips and fruit teas that I have been dragging around Europe are surplus to requirements. I just drink my loose green tea, which I have plenty of, as I only put a pinch in a cup. I can't think of a better place to leave my teabags than with someone who appreciates tea. I leave a little note with 'Enjoy,' and go down and pay for my room and go to the bus stop.

I walk straight to the bus stop without getting lost, which is a blessing. The landscape out of the window is not great as we go through a few dull towns. I read *Homeless, Free as a bird* by Clive Ward on my Kindle.

I have put my rucksack in the hold under the bus and feel a little weird about not being able to see it. It's been in my sight on every journey, or locked in a room or padlocked in a container. I feel a sense of panic that someone might get off a stop and take it, even though there's only four of us on the bus. So, I change seats to where I can see the bags when the storage door opens and so I can see if anyone takes it and now I can relax.

The bus pulls into Ljubljana airport. I had no idea this place has an airport. Interesting if I want to come back to this part of the world.

My book is good. I am so engrossed that I look out of the window for the first time as we pull into Ljubljana bus station. I am a bit confused. It took an hour and a half going to Bled, so I was expecting another half an hour on the bus, but there is the terminal café that I drank awful tea in two days ago. I get off quickly and get my bag before someone else does.

It's 11.00 am and I check the trains. The next one is at 2.45 pm which is a long wait, so I go to the bus station and buy a ticket for a bus that leaves at 1.15 pm, which is still a bit of a wait, but not as much as the train. I could have got the train for free, but that would use a whole day's travel for a small train ride, so I was going to pay for this journey, anyway. It makes no difference financially if I go by bus or train. I need to start planning my journey home so that I know how many travel days I need to keep on my Interrail ticket. I will need a day to get to Budapest, if that's where I am going.

I spent 60 cents on the loo. You need a separate budget just for wees.

It feels strange being back in Ljubljana. I was only here for three days, but it feels very familiar. Especially the traffic light crossings that make the funny click-click to say that it's safe to cross.

I finish my book; it was very enjoyable. It's fiction, but it felt like it could have been real.

I spot a Loving Hut, a vegan eatery, over the road from the bus station. There is one in Brighton, where Liam lived, that I have passed and not gone in. I still have a long wait, so that seems like a good option. I could have eaten here when I was staying at the hostel, what a shame.

The food looks and smells great. It has a help-yourself salad bar which is my favourite kind of food, but I am still full from my omelette. That's a contradiction in a vegan eatery. I get a Cockta herbal coke that I had in the vegan place in Bled yesterday, and a slice of something that looks like a cross between a flapjack and a biscuit, with a thick layer of chocolate on it. I carry my glass, bottle, and biscuit thing outside, but I knock a chair over first with my backpack and scatter a cushion. I put everything down on the table and pick the chair up, then I nearly topple over with the weight of my bag, trying to pick up the cushion. No one comments or comes to assist. Not the friendliest of places, which is unusual for a vegan establishment. That's what I loved about my café; the customers were so friendly and chatty. That's not the case here.

I sit on the outside chairs where I can see the bus stop. I was going to save my biscuit, but it's gone, it was quite yummy. I am nervous about drinking the whole bottle of cola as I have two and a half-hours on a bus. Even if they have a loo, I'm not too keen on using it after reading the book that I just finished. You'll have to read it to find out.

I can feel myself unwinding another notch. Maybe I learned some lessons in Bled. The two-hour wait isn't bothering me. I am in transit, off to explore Zagreb, which I know almost nothing about. It's in Croatia, so a new currency and new language which will be interesting. I have booked two nights and I will know when I am there if I want another. I was thinking of spending longer in places to slow myself down. It looks like a nice place from the photos, but as I know already, they don't always show the truth. I loved the guesthouse that I just left and will give it a glowing report on Tripadvisor. I couldn't fault anything.

I text Phil my location from the bus stop over the road. He says he can picture me now as he looks at Google Maps as well. I am happy for Phil, as his eldest daughter, Becky, is home for a couple of weeks. Maria, his youngest and Becky get on so well. The girls and Phil have a great sense of humour and there will be lots of laughter in the house.

Laughter is what got me through my marriage. Between the bullying and fear, there was laughter. Sometimes when things have turned bad, you either laugh or cry and, as incredible as it sounds, laughter did get us through sometimes. It was his sense of humour that attracted me to him in the first place. Some of the situations were so bad, it was impossible to know how to resolve them. Laughter is a passage from here to there. A way of moving on, and if you can laugh, it means the worst is behind you, without having to have a conversation about why the argument or situation happened in the first place. As in most relationships, you have patterns of behaviour that are weaved in over time, and you learn how to negotiate difficult situations and move forward.

There's a lot of unhealthy bonding in a relationship of abuse. Especially if you don't tell anyone outside what is happening, which I didn't. I couldn't keep some of it from my mum, but it was a huge shock to even my closest friends when I told them what I had been going through. I still haven't told all my story, only snippets. So, you only have each other, and each experience, even if it's bad, bonds you together even further.

You have to look at your situation and work out how to handle it. I was in a marriage that didn't turn out how I hoped it would. I wasn't treated well or loved as I deserved to be.

But in between that, we muddled along. Sometimes we got on really well. We went months sometimes with hardly a raised voice and that gave me hope that it would all be OK in the future, that maybe we had turned a corner. But I always knew in my heart that it was the calm before the storm and it was always difficult to totally relax, even if everything seemed good.

My main concern and my only priority were my children. They had to have the best life that I could give them with the situation that I was in.

I could have left. It's very difficult to explain why I didn't. There are so many reasons. Financial reasons, can I survive with less money coming in and raise the kids, pay the bills, and keep a roof over our heads? Do I want to admit that I failed? My parents' marriage failed, although that was due to my dad's affairs. I didn't want to fail as well.

A big reason was owning up to myself, let alone to other people, what was actually going on in my marriage. I was seriously in denial, but that was a way of protecting myself. It's not an easy conversation to have with yourself about how bad your marriage is and whether you should admit it's awful and leave. I couldn't imagine telling anyone else what my marriage was like. The only control that I had left was if I didn't tell anyone, then no one could interfere. Those are all good reasons to consider.

But the main reason I didn't leave was to protect my children. I decided to stay and try to control what I could, which I could do while we all lived in the same house. He would have had the children on his own at weekends if we separated, and I definitely didn't want this to happen. If we were still a family unit, the kids were part of a family, rather than having their parents separated.

So, I tried hard to give the kids an amazing childhood. Better than average, a fantastic childhood. I did the best that I could, and I did enjoy their company. They were cute children and all so close in age. We had a family holiday every year, whether we could afford it or not. The credit cards got bashed. We were always frugal when we got there. We went self-catering and had breakfast before we left in the mornings. There were always biscuits in my bag and I always carried water, so we didn't need to buy any. And we had only one main meal a day out.

We went to America three or four times when the kids were small to stay with my sister Susan. So, free accommodation, and she was always very generous and treated us to meals at home and meals out, and she bought the kids gifts. We also went to Majorca twice, Gran Canaria, Dublin, and Rosslare.

We also camped a lot, somewhere close, sometimes only three miles away, sometimes a bit further. Liam swam the length of an outdoor pool on a camping trip when he was about five.

The whole family enjoyed camping, the kids getting fresh air and freedom and lots of space. The kids loved the play parks. I did much less cooking. My mum even got the bus to visit us for a BBQ at the tent if we had camped close. These were fun times. The kids had freedom and drove around on the campsites on their scooters or played ball. We played a lot of cards. They were good times, as long as we didn't take too much drink. I preferred sites with no pub so he could only drink what we had brought with us. I had to drink my quota, so that there wasn't any spare for him to finish off. I drank more than I should have during my marriage.

I have spoken to the kids and they say they had a great childhood filled with holidays, great birthday parties, laughter, and good memories. So, I did well. Maybe they had a better childhood because I overcompensated and made aspects of their childhood even more positive than they might have been? I doubt that's true. Nothing makes up for a life of eggshells, but maybe the eggshells were not always as obvious to them as they were to me.

I was a good mum. I am not egotistical and don't sell myself well to anyone, but I do acknowledge I was a good mum. I am feeling a bit emotional writing this whilst drinking my cola opposite the Ljubljana bus station. I took hours and hours of camcorder videos, 32 tapes in all, proving that I was a good mum and the kids were having a good childhood. The proof is right there in the tapes.

I have a clip of the three of them, aged five, four, and two, sitting around the kitchen table, decorating fairy cakes that we had made. Liam says to Ciara in his Suffolk accent, 'Your cake is sooooo bootiful,' and it melts my heart every time I watch it. The cake in question is an inch deep in icing sugar and sprinkles. Those are the moments that make being a parent priceless and there were lots and lots of them. Birthday parties that were full of Easter egg hunts, musical statues, crafts. The kids went home sweaty and happy and we did it three times a year, for years and years. At one of the parties, Aidan sang the whole of 'Happy Birthday' in German. I asked him if he was in the wrong class, as he was supposed to be studying French and everyone laughed. The children were so much fun.

I learnt how to be a good mum from my own mum, who had similar challenges to me, with an alcoholic husband. My birthday parties growing up were always great fun, with lots of laughter, friends, and food. I just did the same for my children. When I was a child, my mum took the three of us off for adventures on the bus, getting off where we wanted to. We even went on walks around our town, and we were allowed to decide whether to turn left or right. We didn't know where we were, but I suspect now that my mum always knew. She was a very calming influence in a sometimes difficult childhood, and she managed somehow to keep a roof over our heads and keep us fed. I think maybe that's where I get my survival skills from.

At 12.45 pm, I walk back across the road and wait for my bus. At 2.00 pm, a bus to Zagreb eventually turns up, but it's the bus before my one. My ticket is only valid for the 1.15 pm and the bus driver won't let me on. I go over to the bus station and ask for an update on when the bus will be here and the man says he doesn't know, I just have to wait. So, I ask for a refund of €15.99 and go and get the train which should leave at 2.45 pm and costs €9.00.

If I had known I would have to wait four hours, I might have done something more impressive than sit at the bus station. It's been a bit frustrating as I could have stayed in Bled a few hours longer. But it's all part of the trip and having time on my own with no distractions to take stock of my life is going to be a positive experience. I have just started a new book on my Kindle, which is looking good: *The Authenticity Project* by Clare Pooley.

The train is cute. It's got little rooms or booths for six people, like in a whodunnit film. It has a long corridor outside the booths. The upholstery is green and matches my bag. This is a two-and-a-half-hour journey, and it's very cheap. I am going to cross the border from Slovenia to Croatia, which is exciting.

The train takes off on time and so far my little room is empty, so I can take my mask off for a bit.

It's a nice ride. There are lots of churches, one very close to the train track and many more scattered over the countryside and perched on hilltops. The train stations all seem to be painted salmon-coloured and are neat and tidy. They even have old trains as ornaments by the stations.

I am not sure if I am in Slovenia or Croatia; the map says that 80% of the trip is in Slovenia. I leave my carriage to stretch my legs and look out of the right-hand window. A river is running parallel with the train track and everything is green and pretty out of the window. Lots of detailed chalet-style houses on the hills with coloured roofs. I sit back down and eat some nuts that I brought from England to curb the hunger and finish my bottle of cola. There are big black clouds in the sky. I hope they are not coming with us.

The train is going fairly slowly, stopping everywhere, but it's very pleasant. I feel chilled despite the delays. I am not anxious about the hostel or what happens next and the book on my Kindle is keeping me entertained between spells of looking out of the window.

I don't think I will know when we have crossed the border. I don't know if I will be able to differentiate between Slovenian and Croatian on the signposts. Probably not.

I fancy chips for tea. I thought I would eat more chips than I have, but I have only had one portion of curly fries with Liam.

It's very quiet when the train stops at a station, just silence. There are no busy roads, nothing industrial, just a little chatter from the station. The train itself is eerily quiet, maybe because it's not an open carriage. We are all in our little rooms.

We must have crossed the border, as two Croatian policemen appear in my booth and want to see my passport. They ask me where I am going, and anywhere else in Croatia that I might visit and for how long. They are very tall and serious in their uniforms. It is a little uncomfortable.

At Dobova, the train stops for ages. I assume the police are checking everyone's passports. I send Phil three words.

We get moving again and another ticket officer wants to see my ticket. But first he wants me to put my mask on. I can't find it. It usually keeps my chin warm or hangs off my ears and now it's gone. This is one time that I need it stuck to my face or I will get a fine. I fluster about and find it under my bag and quickly put it on. He looks at my ticket and moves on.

We arrive in Zagreb and I step out onto a wide view with tram lines and a huge statue of a man on a horse. Behind it is a big yellow building with a dome. This is an impressive entrance to Zagreb.

It's an easy 10-minute walk to my hostel. The roads are organised and long and straight so it's easy enough to find and well signposted when I get there. Dots Hostel is clearly marked with a hanging sign.

It's a little strange, a bit like going for an interview in an office block. I have to be buzzed in and climb the stairs, then get to a reception area. It's all very clean and white and swish, with lovely artwork of Zagreb on the walls. My room is perfect. It is very big and spotless, with a pretty blue pillow, and it's just for me. I have a bathroom next door, which is also clean and new.

I go and ask if there's a kettle, but the receptionist explains that there were earthquakes recently and the kitchen got damaged, so there's no breakfast either. That is very annoying for me, although probably more distressing for them. But I chose this place because it offered breakfast and the computer allowed me to book and pay for the breakfast. So, that's disappointing. She offers to bring some hot water for my tea which is the best I am going to get. I have a much-needed cup of green tea and go straight out to explore, with the map the receptionist has given me.

There is evidence of the earthquake with lots of broken buildings and repair work going on. There are some big buildings, which are quite majestic. I walk out of the main shops and find an older part of town on a higher level, up some steep steps. There seems to be a lot of history. The tram lines freak me out, I don't know if I should walk across them or not. So, I wait to see what someone else does. They survive, and don't get electrocuted, so I walk across the lines.

After wandering around for a while, I get takeaway chips and sit in the park to eat them. They are delicious. I am very tired and a bit done with history and big buildings. This is so far from Bled, it's almost another planet, and I am not sure I like it. I walk back to my room and settle for the night.

Zagreb
Sunday 16th August

I am woken by the sound of an angry man shouting at the receptionist. The whole hostel is on one floor and my room is nearest the reception area. I obviously have no idea what the problem is as I can't understand a word, but he is cross and she is defending herself very well. I feel safe in my locked room, but still a little anxious.

When the shouting subsides, I go ask for more hot water, as I need a cup of tea. The receptionist kindly brings me another cup of hot water for my green tea and I eat the bruschetta biscuits that I bought in the supermarket in Ljubljana. It really is a shame there isn't any breakfast here.

It's gone one o'clock before I go to sleep as I have been researching where to go next. I just can't decide. I can't deny that I am a bit tired and dizzy with making decisions. The plan was to go to Budapest and I have found a train, and I also spoke to the lady in the train station yesterday. But, after spending time here in Zagreb, I just don't fancy another big city. I wandered around aimlessly yesterday, crossing busy junctions and looking at some quite impressive buildings and just not having any enthusiasm to find out what they were all about. I am a bit building-ed out. I need to get back to nature. I knew at the beginning of this trip that big cities didn't interest me much.

I originally wanted to go to Tapolca in Hungary, one of my lockdown-researched places. But it's a difficult place to get to and there were only two accommodations available on the internet: one with a 4.4 rating and awful reviews, and the other for €367 a night. So, I won't be staying at either of those. I have googled what to do near Lake Balaton, which is near Tapolca as a lake is always nice. I find some accommodation for €50 a night, 500 metres from the edge of the lake, so that's where I decide to go next and book it before I go to sleep, so that I can relax.

So, what to do in Zagreb with my one full day? Out of the many things you can do in a city, I decide to visit a cemetery. I know ... bit weird. There are parks and museums but I don't fancy them and the cemetery looks very interesting.

I decide to walk the 45 minutes as it's very doable and I have no idea how to buy a ticket for the buses. It's a good choice as it's a nice walk up a tree-lined avenue. I see a corner shop and I am really hungry, I need some supplies in case there is nowhere to buy food at the cemetery. Probably not, I don't think it's a tourist attraction even though there was a leaflet telling me about it.

So, in this very small corner shop I pick up hummus and crisps, which I really fancy, and a couple of lovely looking peaches and some grapes. I take my basket to the till. It's a little busy and there is a bit of a queue.

The lady rings it all and asks me for money, but of course, I can't understand her. I can't see the till's computer screen because it's tilted at the wrong angle. So, I don't know how much it is. I sorted out all my money last night. I have some bits the kids gave me from their trip around Europe and I sorted them all out so that I had some cash today. I hand her the biggest note that I have, a 200 note which I think is worth £26.00. She throws it back at me in disgust. Surely my grapes, peach, crisps, and hummus doesn't cost more than £26.00? Maybe she doesn't have any change, which seems odd because they are very busy. I get out another note, a 10. She says 'Kuna, not koruna,' and I realise my mistake. I am giving her the wrong currency. I am not giving her Croatian kuna, but Czech koruna. The notes look very similar and sound similar, and I obviously didn't do a very good job of organising them last night.

I fumble in my bag for kuna, but I still don't know how much I owe her. I have my sunglasses on which don't help as everything is dark, so I take them off but then I can't see anything now as they are prescription sunglasses. I try to tell her that I can't see the screen, but she doesn't understand and is getting very cross. I point again at the screen and she understands, at last. It's 30.48 kuna. Out of my see-through money bag, I get out 40 kuna. I don't have any coins. She can see my bag has no coins in it but she still keeps making circle shapes with her finger and thumb. I keep dangling my bag in front of her, showing her that I don't have any coins, so she throws the 10 back to me and then the receipt.

Flustered and embarrassed, I walk out of the shop. I am so dithery sometimes, and I know that drives people mad. It was entirely my own fault. You should have the right currency when you go in a shop and it's not her fault that she doesn't speak English in a residential corner shop in her own city. I pack my bits into my bag, it's quite a squeeze with the big bag of crisps.

I cross the big main road and get on the road that I need and stop. I still feel a bit flustered, and hungry. I get my peach out of the bag, lean against a wall and take a deep breath. It will all be OK. The peach is huge and delicious and drips down my arm. I wish you could buy them like this at home. After de-stressing and finishing the peach, I start walking again.

When I get to the cemetery, and I am blown away by the size of it. It's 500 metres long, which I knew, as it said so in the leaflet, but to see a wall that long and tall in real life is incredible. And there are green domes every so often along the wall. I don't see anywhere to pay so I just go in and it's so peaceful. Only one or two people are wandering about. This was a good decision, just what I needed, a break from the city.

There is so much marble. Every grave is a work of art, with statues and huge marble headstones. I notice the bigger ones are family graves, so strange to know exactly where you will end up at the end of your life. Some even have the name and date and a dash, so they will fill in the death day when it arrives. I don't know if that's spooky or not.

I have no idea where I will end up, and I have no idea where some of my family is. I wonder if it's a comfort knowing you will be laid to rest with your family and it will be respectful and right? I wonder if you can get on with your life better, facing death and its inevitability face-on.

The cemetery is huge, I have never seen anything like it. Rows and rows and rows of tombstones as far as you can see. My mum would love it here. She loves a good cemetery. I am hungry and I need to find a spot and eat some of my picnic. It's a strange place to eat, but I am sure they don't mind. I sit down in a quiet secluded spot by a war memorial, which is fascinating and quite moving. The crisps are very noisy and it feels a bit disrespectful, but I am so hungry. I eat what I need and put the hummus and crisps back in my bag. I am not going to be able to see all of this, it would take days, but I do spend a fair bit of time wandering around.

I don't come from a religious family or a big family. My mum has religion in her life and has attended the Salvation Army for as long as I can remember, and it's important to her. It was also a big part of my sister's life growing up. We all enjoyed the community and friendship of the Salvation Army. It was just at the end of our road, and whilst I only went to a handful of services, I did enjoy all the events. At my funeral, I want 'Count your Blessings' sung, which is a song that I remember fondly from the Salvation Army.

I have my own religious views, as we all do. At my funeral I want someone to read out the poem, 'Don't stand at my grave and weep. I am not there,' which is a bit hypocritical, walking around all these graves. These people obviously don't share that thought. These graves are statements of wealth and are very well-tended with fresh flowers and candles.

It's a lovely place, and I am so glad that I came to visit.

On the walk back, I stop at a park, which I notice from the road. It's so cute, a real little find. It's the brightest open-air café that I have ever seen, with vivid pinks, purples, natural green from the lush grass, and added green from decorations. There are clusters of tables and chairs on paving slabs, so each one is a little world of its own. All the chairs in the park have brightly coloured cushions and a parasol, random plants and wooden plaques saying, 'I Love You,' which I notice is photographed a lot. I take a photo myself and send it to Phil. Someone has spray-painted a bike. It's utterly cute, and I love it.

It's really hot, and I order a Sicilian lemonade and sit down. It's not as zingy as the lemonade in Venice, but it's very welcome in the heat. I can't stop looking around. It's such a brightly coloured, cute outdoor space. Hippy dippy, bright, and colourful. There is music playing, and it's perfect, a bit of a beat but not overpowering.

I notice that the Sicilian lemonade is ironically made with soft Devon spring water, which makes me laugh. It's travelled as far as I have to get to Zagreb. Mind you, it probably didn't come via Ljubljana or Venice. It costs 20 kuna, which I think is £2.60. But who knows, my financial brain is not in gear today.

Reluctantly, after about an hour or so, I leave this pretty place to go and see the town. If I lived locally, I think that I would spend a lot of time here. I would come with Tami, she would love it here as well. I walk past the cathedral and go up to the old part of town again and have a good wander around. I look for somewhere to eat, there are lots and lots of places but I don't feel like sitting at a busy pavement restaurant. It's too noisy and expensive and it doesn't feel right.

So, I go back to my room and have a cup of tea and the rest of the biscuits from Ljubljana. The lady has left the kettle plugged in at the reception area so that I can use it whenever I want. She has no idea how much I appreciate that.

I chill. It's been a good day, and I have seen everything that I want to see in Zagreb. I spend a lot of time chilling and planning the next leg of my journey. I think I can fit Český Krumlov in. It was high on my list at the beginning, but it has always looked complicated to get to. But after some research, I think it's possible and it can be a nice stop on my way back to England, as soon I will have to stop travelling right and turn left.

The plan at the moment is Zagreb to Gyenesdiás, which is near Lake Balaton, so that I can go to Tapolca. Then to Brno, more because of where it is, but it looks nice as well. Then Brno to Český Krumlov and possibly Mainz because I can go on the pretty part of the train along the Rhine and then the Eurostar home.

I will have to quarantine now, Boris says. All three Eurostar points; Belgium, France, and Amsterdam are now on the quarantine list which is a bit annoying. Actually, very annoying, but I chose to travel in these strange times, so I can't complain.

I have been talking to Ciara and she has a holiday to use up. She wanted to visit Liam in France, but now there is a 14-day quarantine and it's not possible, as she needs to be back at work and can't spend time quarantining. So, she is going to Germany, and we might meet in Mainz. That's something to look forward to and so funny that we will both be in Germany at the same time as it wasn't planned like that. I don't have a burning desire to go to Germany, but it's a huge country and I need to cross it to get back to England. I think there are lots of pretty places to visit, some of them in the Black Forest, in the southwest. But I don't want to go south after Český Krumlov, which is why I thought I would go to the Rhine.

I pop out to get a sweetcorn for tea from a street trader that I saw yesterday in the park in the next green square. I don't take my map or phone or bag, which feels very strange, as it's the first time I have been outside since I left Cornwall without my bag and phone. It's surprising how quickly a place can feel familiar. Except Venice.

I take the sweetcorn home and eat it in my room. It's delicious. Grilled on the hot plate in the park and sweet and delicious.

I get an early night and hopefully the 9.48 am train to Gyenesdiás tomorrow.

Croatia to Hungary
Monday 17th August

The lady at the train station ticket office looks at my scrap of paper that says Gyenesdiás and pulls a funny face as she doesn't know where it is. That's not a good start. I get my rail planner app out and enlighten her. She can only sell me a ticket to Nagykanizsa, then I have to buy another one. That makes sense as I am going to a different country. I am off to Hungary. I am not using the Interrail ticket today as I need the day for Germany and the train tickets will be cheaper here.

I have a headache which started last night and now she tells me there is a bus between two stations that I can't remember the name of and hands me my ticket. It was going to be a tight connection between the trains, so now with a bus it's not going to happen. But I have got to the train station early so hopefully it will all work out.

I am a bit worried now, as I can't understand the announcements on the train, so I won't know when to get off. It's going to be a nervous ride and my rucksack is better suited to trains than buses. I also feel a little sick. I do hope I am not going to be ill. I get travel sick on buses, so I am not looking forward to that but I just have to get on with it.

Despite there being hundreds of places to eat in Zagreb, I didn't eat well. There was almost too much choice and I will try to get a proper meal and some nutrients in Gyenesdiás. This might be a long, difficult day.

The train has six berth pods again, and this time I share with a man from Hungary. A real live person to talk to. He helps me with the language difficulties when the conductor explains the bus situation and which carriage to get back on with the next train.

We get off the train and a line of us walks across the train track. I have never done this before, except near St Ives and there is a specific place to walk. I have to step down onto the track and with my little legs and a big rucksack, I feel a bit unbalanced but I don't fall, so I am happy.

The four-bus convoy of train passengers heads off into Eastern European suburbia, passing lots of half-built houses. My Hungarian friend had explained on the train in broken English that once your house has its outside layer on, you have to pay tax. Many house owners just don't finish their rendering and leave it brick. It sounds like a strange system to me. So, the houses we pass on the bus all look unfinished, but with mature shrubs and flowers that must have been growing for years.

We stop at Vrbovec train station, where I thought we were getting off. The bus doors open and no one moves. The Hungarian man is a few seats back and is going the same way as me. He doesn't get off, so I stay put. Then we are told that there is a change of plan and we are going to the next station. The poor conductor is having to go around and explain the situation to everyone. He is very kind though. He tells me that the lads that were in the next booth on the train are going to Budapest, which is where I am going for part of the journey and to just follow them when we stop. I wonder if I have made the right decision not to go to Budapest. I am on the train to take me straight there.

We pass a beautiful cemetery. They do look after their loved ones in this part of the world. The church is painted orange and the graves are bursting with flowers. In some way, it's more impressive than yesterday's cemetery. No, not more impressive, more loved.

We get back on the train at Koprivnica, but we don't go anywhere. Hungary police are doing passport control. The uniformed policeman holds my passport for five or 10 minutes, and it feels like an eternity. He keeps swiping it on his machine and tapping the screen with the edge of my passport. There is either a problem with the machine or with me.

Eventually, he hands it back. I am sharing my new six-berth pod with a young Croatian man who speaks perfect English with an American accent, which he later explains is because he watched a lot of American movies growing up.

The train hasn't moved yet. I guess they are checking all the passports.

Then another much more severe-looking policeman, with a gun on his hip, wants to see my passport. He asks me lots of questions: where am I going, for how long, where did I go before this? I've answered all these questions before crossing into another country. They are normal questions. I'm OK, I tell myself. He asks how long I was in Croatia, and where I was before this and I say 'Ljubljana.' He walks away with my passport. Now I'm worried. He returns with his colleague and he asks the same questions. In the confusion, my brain goes into meltdown with nerves, I have forgotten to say I was in Lake Bled. He hasn't heard of it, his English is not good, so he can't understand me. My new friend translates and says Bled is in Slovenia. Then he asks where I was before that and where before that. When did I leave England? I am worn out and my brain is shutting down with these intense questions. I sense they think I am making up random countries and it's all a lie. Then I have a brainwave and get out my Interrail ticket. It has everywhere that I have been recorded and I don't have anything to hide. Hopefully, it will clarify everything better than the mumbled jumble coming out of my mouth. It might not be the right thing to do, but it's best to be honest. I don't know why they are so worried. Have I been to a country that has COVID-19? Am I not allowed in Hungary? They both look at my ticket and one walks away again. I think I am going to get thrown off. I don't know why. But this isn't feeling good.

He returns and gives me my passport and ticket back and says thank you. Phew.

The train stays on the platform for another 45 minutes while they check on everyone. Three lads walk past our window, they have been thrown off. The train is still on schedule. I guess they factor these timings in. My friend tells me that trains are cheaper than buses, which I have found out already at Ljubljana. He says that there is no money being put into the railways in Croatia or Hungary. The buses are often faster, which is why the bus bit I had to do didn't slow us down like it might have in England.

We continue, and I get off at Nagykanizsa and buy the onward ticket to Gyenesdiás. The station is really old and tatty, but not in a bad way. It's very humble and I feel like I have stepped back in time.

I have no idea how much my ticket cost as we have a new currency now. I have to walk on the train track again. I feel a little lost. Not knowing the language is OK if people speak English, but I seem to be drifting into non-English-speaking countries and struggling to communicate with people. I hold my ticket out for the man with the red hat to read my destination. He nods, so I get on. The Interrail app says it leaves at 1.19 pm, and so does my ticket and I feel confident that I am on the right train.

I distract myself with a bag of grapes that I bought in that corner shop by the cemetery. They are all different sizes, some big, some tiny. I have not seen grapes like this since I was a child; everything is so uniform now in the shops. Then I eat my hummus and crisps. I was going to read my Kindle but what with chatting with the Hungarian man and the Croatian man, and the custom fuss, I haven't had time. I am feeling more relaxed now. It's been a long journey, which is why I nearly didn't come here. This is the fourth train, plus one bus, and now one more train after this.

I have three stops till Balatonszentgyorgy: two beginning with Z and one with a V. This is followed by a three-minute run for the next, and last, train of the day. The landscape is very flat. There is a huge road project going on, miles of new road being laid. Hungary feels like a richer country than Croatia.

I make the connection easily as it's on the next platform, easy in these tiny stations. I just walk across the tracks again, although this time there are sort of paths; raised bits between the tracks. Why bother with all those stairs and subways? Just walk across. There is a man or woman with a red hat at all the stations trying to make sure people don't get run over by the trains.

The platform at Balatonszentgyorgy is cute, painted nicely with lots of hanging baskets and no graffiti. I am feeling quite optimistic. It's been a whirlwind kind of day but 16 minutes and I should be there. This train is funky, it has a few steps and the middle bit looks like a tube with poles to hold on to.

I get off at Gyenesdiás. It has literally one train track, so the trains must have to wait somewhere to pass, and just one small building, which looks empty. There isn't a platform as such, it's a brick path that runs along the side of this single track. You could almost mistake it for a cycle path. The single train track is so small, and the path is wider. But it's so green and lush and the air feels fresh, and it's *so* quiet. I like it.

I can't get Wi-Fi but I did take a screenshot of the journey from the train to the guesthouse. It's very straightforward.

As I get closer, I am looking at the door numbers when I see a naked man on his doorstep, holding onto the wall with one hand to steady himself and trying to flick his swimming trunks off his foot. He must be too fat to bend down, and thankfully too fat for me to see anything. It's all well covered despite his nakedness. Luckily, the house that I am going to is a few doors up.

It's a nice-looking house; quite big, lots of space and the landlady seems to live in an extension out the front. I take a quick shower and go out to explore. I want to see the lake.

The road that I am on is like posh suburbia. It's a wide road and seems to be the only one going to the lake, past the train station again, over the train track. The houses have pools and sunbathing areas. It's all very nice.

I pass a small market area, and a lady has peaches. I desperately want one, as I am really hungry. Hungry in Hungary, I laugh to myself, but I don't have any currency so I can't buy one, which is a huge shame as I love peaches. I need to find an ATM.

It's not far to Lake Balaton, which is why I booked this room. I can see bits of the water, but there are buildings in the way. It looks like you have to pay to go into a children's area. There is a turnstile and a pay kiosk like the entrance to a theme park, and through it, I can see families and people in swimming costumes, and there is lots of noise. Not what I want, so I go for a stroll and try to get to the lake another way. There is a tall fence and no way to get near the water. This is very strange and not what I imagined.

I am going to have to investigate. It's 3.30 pm and I don't have much time to do anything else. I go to the kiosk and try to ask what all this is about, but the lady working there doesn't speak English, so she goes to find someone who does. He manages to tell me there is another beach two miles away, but I will need a bike. His English isn't good enough to tell me why I need a bike and I just don't know what to do. This is a million miles away from what I had pictured in my head.

I can see from the information on the wall that it shuts at 7.00 pm, so I don't have much choice. I have to go in or go home. I wasn't expecting to go to a lake that shut. I have been travelling all day and I need to get to the lake. I pay on my card, it's 1,000 HUF (Hungarian Forints). I have no idea what that is, but it's busy so it can't be a huge amount.

I walk in and it's like entering a parallel universe. There are so many people squished into a relatively small space. There are swimming costumes, adults and children, candy floss, stalls with brightly coloured beach stuff, and lots of noise from the kids and music playing. I am stunned. It's completely awful and I hate it.

This is absolutely as far from what I imagined as it could possibly be. I thought I would sit by a peaceful lake and read my book. That is obviously not going to happen here. I weave across the grass between families sunbathing, kids playing, balls flying overhead and music ruining the air. It's packed solid. I get to the edge of the lake and it has a concrete wall, no grass. It's like the edge of a swimming pool, and it's full of people swimming and enjoying themselves.

And the water is murky, like a giant muddy puddle. Why are they all in it? They will come out filthy. I stand mesmerised at the sight in front of me. To be fair, everyone except me seems to be having a wonderful time.

Oh dear.

I collect my three words to send to Phil when I have Wi-Fi. I don't know how much he will be able to see from home. I am very hungry and there are lots of food outlets here, obviously. There is a captive audience and the prices are probably ridiculous, but I have to eat.

I notice a fridge full of drinks and scan the prices. I see it's 590 HUF for a Coke. Phew, it cost the equivalent of two bottles of Coke to get in, so that's not too bad.

The food is typical feed-hungry-family food: burgers, pizzas, gyros. And the menus are in Hungarian. I wander up and down, looking at the menus and at people's plates. I stop. I have looked at all the food places and I have to make a decision. More options aren't going to appear if I walk up and down again. I am so hungry I can hardly think.

I find a place with photos of the food which is a big help. Luckily, the girl speaks English and reluctantly, I order chips and salad. That's as good as I'm going to get. The food is OK; it cost 1400 HUF, three bottles of Coke, so that's OK, but I did want something warm and comforting. I am annoyed with myself for not eating better in Zagreb when I was surrounded by restaurants. This is the third day in a row with bad food choices. Chips one night in Zagreb and a piece of sweetcorn the next. Now chips and salad. I will get ill if I don't start eating well.

I can't get Wi-Fi at my table. My data doesn't work and I couldn't get Wi-Fi at the guesthouse either, the code wouldn't work. I feel cut off and fed up.

How did I get this so wrong?

After my mediocre meal, I go nearer to the entrance and the Wi-Fi that came with the entrance fee pings in. I chat to Phil and all is OK again. I am a bit frazzled and tell him about my fuss with customs, and that I have no Wi-Fi, no phone signal, and no local money. But it feels better to have a chat and we laugh about where I have ended up.

I decide to get out of this horrendous place and go find the other lake. Two miles is doable, and what else am I going to do?

It's a lovely straight path that must follow the lake, which you can't see from the path. There are trees all along it, it's very nice. I nearly get flattened by a constant flow of bikes. It's like trying to walk on the M25.

Guess what? I have to pay again. It's 650 HUF this time, so less, but it's 5.15 pm now, and this closes at 7.00 pm, but I might as well just go in. It looks much quieter. Fewer primary colours, fewer half-naked families, and no music.

It has a path straight to the water, rather than tripping over bodies on the grass. It's much smaller, and it has a tiny beach, not a swimming pool edge. I have my swimming costume on and I really want to go for a swim. It feels safe here and there are reeds on either side of the beach area and somewhere safe to put my bag.

I think I have worked out what's happened. The lake is inaccessible because of the reeds. So, someone bought the land, made it people-friendly and now charges people to come in and use the lake. I don't know for sure, but that's what it looks like to me.

I walk into the water with my clothes on. The water is up to my ankles and when I look down, I can't see my feet. The water is so dirty that I can't see my feet in six inches of water. I am not swimming in that. So, I sit down in a seating area and chill. It's OK here, it has a nice feel to it. I do some people-watching for a while. A few people are going in and out of the water. It has a much calmer feel and I am glad that I came here. Then a big black cloud and wind appears and everyone starts to pack up. I do the same. That was a short stay.

The clouds follow me but I manage to walk faster and get home without getting wet but it was a chilly walk back. Everyone who left the beach walked to the train station, well, stood on the path where the trains come by. It's a great system.

I need to get some money out to pay the landlady as she wants cash. Plus, I need to have money for tomorrow, so I go to the ATM that I saw outside the entrance to the noisy area. I don't feel comfortable using it as it's one of those stand-alone ones that looks like you can pick it up and walk away with it. But I haven't seen anything else. Someone is using it, so I wait a polite distance away and I don't speak the language but I can tell that the receipt has come out and no money ... hmmm. I walk back to the house without any cash.

I knock on the landlady's door, and I feel like I am disturbing her. There doesn't seem to be any other guests here, just me and her. I can't get the Wi-Fi to work, so she shuffles into the house in her slippers with me, gets my phone working and goes again. She's not very friendly. There are no towels left out for me, so I have to use my hand towel to shower. I got a towel in Zagreb in the hostel and it was half this price. The kitchen doesn't look like it's been used in months, the fridge is turned off. She hasn't shown me the kitchen or asked if she can help with anything. Its bottom row hospitality here.

And the toilet ... well, there's no flush. I stare at it and just can't work it out. Then I realise that the handle is the actual water system, you have to open the valve to get water as there's no cistern. The shower cubicle is dark as it's up the far end of the skinny room. When you close the shower curtain, which is necessary or the floor will get soaking wet, it's very dark and you can't see what you are doing. The toilet is at an angle so that you can walk past it to the shower. It's all a bit odd.

I would love a cup of tea, but I can't find a kettle in the kitchen and I have looked in every single cupboard.

At least I have Wi-Fi now, so I work out the currency. I have spent 3,000 Hungarian Forints since arriving, which is about £8.00, on dinner and two entrance fees, so that's not bad. The guesthouse is €50 a night, which in comparison feels an awful lot.

I go to sleep, at least the bed is comfy.

Gyenesdiás
Tuesday 18th August

Last night I googled where in this tiny little suburb there might be an ATM. I found somewhere, but it only had a location, not where it is, like in a shop or on a wall. So I leave the house at 8.00 am to go find it. It's in the opposite direction, which is a shame as the train is 10 minutes away. I walk and walk and it's not where it said it was on the map. I don't have any Wi-Fi in Hungary, so I can't research anymore, and there's no one about on the streets. It's a very strange place.

Before I left, I ate one of the cereal bars that I brought from home and the rest of the grapes. The dinner yesterday wasn't very filling, and I only had a few peanuts last night.

There's a signpost back to the lake, so I follow that. I spend half an hour wandering around a Hungarian housing estate and end up back at the machine down at the lake entrance. I have to use the machine that the lady didn't get her money out of yesterday. Someone is in front of me using it and it works, so fingers crossed, I am going to go for it.

Stupid me, I didn't work out how much to get out when I had Wi-Fi last night. So, I get half of what I think I need, and hoping maybe there's somewhere in Tapolca. The machine gives me loads of bright yellow notes which have '5,000 Forint' written on them. It feels like monopoly money.

I have enough to buy a train ticket to Tapolca now, which was my aim. I can't imagine that they take cards, not at a single-track train station. I catch the 8.57 am train to Tapolca and I am excited to go and see the place that I googled during lockdown.

The train is so cute, it looks like it belongs in a museum. It's orange and red on the outside and has orange and brown chairs with metal legs so you can see underneath. The whole carriage looks ancient, but I love it. This is real travelling, being so far away from the big cities and in a completely different country. This is exactly what I was hoping to find, some character. I am already pleased that I didn't go to Budapest.

I get off at Tapolca but get confused and take the wrong road off the roundabout. I did have the sense to take a photo of the area map near the train station, so I correct myself and walk into another picture postcard.

I am going to be here all day, I think, which is lovely. Right now, I need to have a wee and eat something. I walk around the town and I can't find a toilet. I do find the tourist information, and a lady there directs me to the loo but the directions take me back to where I was already and I need a 200 Forint coin. I don't have any coins so I can't get in. Instead, I look for somewhere to eat where I can use the loo before I wet myself. I find a pub but they don't open till 11.30 am.

At last I find a place that does toasties, and I order a cheese one. I need something substantial and warm. I order a pot of tea as well and go to look for the loo. I walk into the kitchen first. The waitress pointed to the door; I can't read "kitchen" or "toilet" in Hungarian and I went in the wrong one. Oops.

When I leave the toilet, I nearly fall off the step that I wasn't expecting. The staff must think I am bonkers.

I have ordered a fruit tea, I can't have another bad tea. When it arrives, it's really cute with lovely china and a slice of lemon in a metal lemon squeezer and a little pot of honey. I drink it as it is, without all the extras, and it's warm and lovely and exactly what I need. I breathe out. I haven't had a warm drink since Zagreb.

When I was at the train station, the inspector wanted to know a time for my return, which was a bit odd and I wasn't sure. So, he put between 4.00 pm and 8.00 pm in his machine. I'm not sure how that helps anyone, but never mind. I now have all day to relax. The toastie is delicious.

Tapolca is a fascinating place. I read a bit last night, and there are caves here, but the lady at the tourist info said she thinks you need a ticket. I will go and check that out before I go back to the pond.

The tickets are selling out of tickets fast but I am in luck. There's quite a queue and I get a ticket for 4.30 pm. I thought I would go straight in or not get one at all, so I can go chill and have a wander and come back later.

It's picturesque here, the pond is so pretty and still and there is a waterwheel, and a waterfall that goes into a stream. Everyone is taking photos, I think we are all tourists. There is a tiny bridge over the stream with love locks on it.

Then I take a walk through the main street with its selection of shops. I see a bank and go in to get the rest of the money out for the guesthouse. There is a queue, and the machine is in the foyer and every time someone comes into the bank, everyone has to move. When it's my turn, I am a bit confused and conscious that everyone behind me wants me to hurry up. I stuff the money the machine gives me, as discreetly as I can into my bag and zip it up.

I walk around taking photos. Then it starts to spit a bit and I get a prime seat at an outdoor café with parasols directly in front of the pond. I order another fruit tea and just sit and look at the pond. I get Wi-Fi at the café and my bank app pings in and tells me that I took out 7,500 Forints at the lake, which my app tells me is €131.41. I only needed to get out €100 for the accommodation.

What a dipstick. I have just got out an additional €224.76 at the bank, on top of the €131.41 at the lake, which I definitely don't need. I am carrying around over €300 in my bag. Oops. You won't be surprised to know I failed my Maths O-level.

I do remember seeing a bureau de change near the tourist information office which might be the answer. A complete waste of money, getting money out at one end of town and exchanging it at the other, but there's not much else I can do. I don't panic though. What's the point? I enjoy my tea and watch the world go by at the edge of this pretty pond and then go to the toilet.

Luckily, it's a big toilet, with the toilet and sink in the same cubicle, and I get all the money out and lay it on the floor and count it. I know … but what else can I do? I can hardly count it at the table. I look online, calmly, to see what it's worth and what the rate is. I must be prepared as I don't want to be ripped off. I decide to turn it into euros. I will need them in Germany and they are always useful, if I don't spend it all, for future trips to Spain.

The man at the bureau de change is not a very pleasant chap, but the figures he gives me are better than I thought I would get, so I get the deal done and decide to forget all about it, no point crying over spilt milk and all that.

The ducks are very entertaining, skimming across the pond, and playing. I sit down on a bench and eat the peach I just bought on the high street. It's delicious and the ducks are so funny. Everyone is watching and filming them. I have never seen ducks playing like that before.

I decide to go get another drink. You can't say I'm not hydrated today. I end up ordering a bowl of Hungarian goulash. I am not even vegetarian now, let alone vegan, but I said I was going to eat what I wanted on this trip. And I am in Hungary and I will only get this one opportunity. Plus, I must eat better as it's all getting a bit sketchy.

The goulash is absolutely delicious. To be fair, there isn't much meat in it. It is more like a big bowl of tasty, delicious soup with some fresh bread which is perfect.

As I have a bit of free time, I wander around looking at the old historic buildings. I stick my head inside a church, and then I head over to the caves.

I get there a bit too early because I am excited. I can't wait to get in, but I would have been better off waiting outside as it is so hot and we are only on the other side of the barrier. The tour is difficult as it's in Hungarian and all I can do is look at the photos on the wall and read the bits written in English on the wall at every stop. It's nice of them to have English on the walls next to the displays, but I know I am missing a lot of information. It's a struggle for all of us. Kids are bored and people wander off to the next displays while the young lad is still talking.

There's a lot of history about World War II medics in the caves. The caves were used to treat people because of the unique air and constant temperature. The geography of the caves and the area is fascinating, too. And the caves are under the ground all over Tapolca and the surrounding area. The tour would have been better if it was half the time.

Then it's time to go down to the caves. The temperature drops as we walk down a path cut out of the rocks and then queue for the boats. I let all the miserable children who are done in from the tour go first. In fact, I let everyone go first. I am not in a hurry and, to be honest, I am not sure what's happening. There hasn't been any explanation, not in English anyway. So, I want to suss it out first.

There is a couple in front of me and no one behind and I step back a bit as if to say, 'I don't want to be in your boat anymore that you want me in it.' But the thought of rowing my own boat makes me nervous. If I was with Phil, he would drive the boat. That's what men do and I would have been perfectly happy with that. But if I want to get in this boat, which is why I am here, I will have to row myself.

I am a little clumsy sometimes and getting in and out of the boat probably worries me the most. I step down into my metal boat which is like a wide metal canoe with the help of the man's hands to steady me as the boat is moving in the water ... and off I go. The walls are so narrow that I just push off the walls with my stick when I crash. I go so slow that it's hardly a crash, more a bump. Being last was a great idea. I let the couple in front move ahead a little, although none of us are going fast.

I stop oaring and let the boat move on its own, occasionally stopping. The ceilings are low, making proper little tunnels of beige limestone. The shallow water is crystal clear and light turquoise. It is so peaceful and I am not scared at all. I am thoroughly enjoying it. Weaving around bends, bumping into walls, trying to take photos with my camera and phone. I can only put photos on Facebook with my phone knowing the camera would take better photos.

It's a real treat. I keep stopping to just enjoy the moment. How often do you get to be in a tin boat in a quiet, peaceful cave with such blue water? I want to enjoy the serenity of it. But I am also having so much fun, rowing my boat round corners and crashing into walls. I laugh a lot. I go back to the end/beginning. I think I have been on a loop, but you would never know. The young lad is sweet and asks if I enjoyed it and helps me out of the boat.

I walked back to the train station with a spring in my step and a smile on my face. I thoroughly enjoyed the whole experience and I'm also chuffed that I did it on my own and I didn't let my nerves stop me. I was so out of my comfort zone, but I put my nerves to one side and got on with it and I had a great time.

I take the right way to the train station, past the bank, that I got the money out that I didn't need, and laugh again.

It's another old train that only has two carriages and the last carriage, where I sit, has a long seat right at the back with a huge window. So, I have a clear view of the station, which is lovely. It has a white station building and a lady in a red hat walking across the small path on the tracks, checking that everyone is OK.

Tapolca is a lovely place to visit. I sit back and look out of the huge window and enjoy the train journey home along the single track. There is lots of greenery and the cycle track runs parallel with the train.

Being on a single track means that, at one point, a signal man pops out of a hut and, after our train has gone by, he moves the track by hand.

The Gyenesdiás platform is silent again. It has to be one of my favourite stations. I like the informality of it, no station to walk through, no people, no staff, you just get off and walk along the lovely, tiled path.

There is nothing to do at the guesthouse so I wash in the dark shower, dry myself with my hand towel and use the loo that I can't flush. That's enough entertainment for one evening.

I would love a cup of tea, but I can't boil any water. I eat a few more nuts from my bag and a drink of fizzy orange that I bought in Tapolca.

After more research, I decide to stop at Znojmo next, rather than Brno, as it's on the way to Český Krumlov, which is where I want to go.

So, I book one night there and then after lots of research, three nights in Český Krumlov. I really fancy a longer stay somewhere and Český Krumlov looks amazing. It's going to be a long journey with lots of changes. I message Phil. I send him the three words for the guesthouse. He can see on the internet the storms that I am experiencing. He says he can see lightning overhead and, at the same time, I hear a crack of thunder. I was so lucky to have missed the rain today. It is raining and thundering quite bad now, but I am indoors and not going out again today. I have really enjoyed myself and I'm looking forward to tomorrow.

Gyenesdiás to Znojmo
Wednesday 19th August

It's 8.33 am and I am on the train as there was nothing to hang around for. I feel like I was robbed at that guesthouse, absolutely no hospitality at all, no kettle, no hot drink, no breakfast, not even a towel, nothing. But I really can't complain, this trip is full of contrasts and I quite like it. And despite the lake not being what I was expecting, I still enjoyed the madness of it and Tapolca was lovely. I feel a new confidence after going in that boat in the caves by myself. It has really boosted me.

I have five trains to get today to arrive in Znojmo. So, I have written them all down on a piece of paper with times so I don't get flustered. Plus, if I get questioned by customs, then I won't look like a dithering wreck. I am leaving Hungary and going to the Czech Republic.

Gyenesdiás was such a strange place. Even on my walk to look for a cash machine, I didn't see any corner shops. It was residential and extremely quiet, with hardly anyone around. I wish I'd had money on me when I saw that tiny market by the campsite. I would have stocked up with fruit, but it seemed to be only open at certain times. And it wasn't there when I walked back last night.

Chilling on the train, I set up my Kindle and look at the views out of the window and remember that I have a squashed, two-week-old 'That's It' fruit bar at the bottom of my bag and eat it for my breakfast.

At Celldomolk, we pull out of the station and go back the way we came. I am now facing backwards and I haven't moved. I check the Interrail planner and wait nervously to see what the next stop is called. I am so pleased to see 'Papa' written on the walls. What a strange name for a place, sounds like an American pizza but it looks nice. There are big dome shelters over the subway, so there's no walking across train tracks here.

I can relax now, and I move to the opposite chair so that I am facing the right way again. There's an hour's wait for a connection at Gyor and I might be able to get something to eat.

The landscape goes flat, but it's still green and the train track is lined with trees and shrubs. I get off at Gyor and it looks interesting just from stepping off the train, I feel that I might want to come back here. The train is right next to the shops, which is great news for me. There are big buildings but they have character and are neat. It feels clean here and, as I cross over the road, there is a lovely tree-lined shopping stretch.

A cute little bakery selling an array of pastries, some sweet and some savoury, tempts me in. I can't read anything. I can only choose by what they look like and I help myself, putting a few on my tray. I am not worrying about ingredients anymore. They are small so I get about six. I get two drinks as I haven't had much liquid today: orange juice for the vitamins and a cream soda just for the coldness, bubbles, and fun. I go to the till and, thankfully, no one else is here. It seems the little pastries are sold by their weight, which is a good idea. The two young girls are funny, watching me struggling to work it out. Then I don't know what money to give them and I give them too much. They laugh and hand it back.

On the walk back, I see a fruit shop, just a tiny shop in an alcove, with fruit on a bench. I get a peach and ask the lady in English, hoping she'll understand, that I want one which is ready to eat now, as I have an unripe one in my bag. The lady is lovely. She understands and offers to wash the peach in the little sink behind her. This has never happened to me before, I don't even wash them a home.

I get back to the station and get on the train just before the doors shut. I sit down and set up my little picnic as I am famished.

I notice on the Interrail planner that we are going to Austria. I can't go to Austria, it's not allowed with COVID-19. I read that on the Interrail Facebook page.

Oh, no ...

Panic sets in. Should I get off? I look on the Interrail app and try to work out which is the last station in Hungary and think through my options. All the trains, whichever way I try, seem to go through Austria and then back out. It doesn't make any sense.

I decide that getting off voluntarily has the same ending as me being thrown off and there is still a possibility that it won't happen. Thankfully, passport control appear from behind me, so I didn't see them coming, meaning I didn't build up any nerves. One man looks at my passport, takes out a piece of paper from his pocket, reads it, and hands me back my passport. That was easy.

I get off at Parndorf train station, Austria. I was expecting a big station but no, I am the only one who gets off. It's in the middle of nowhere, two platforms and not a soul in sight. No staff, no digital displays, nothing.

Just silence. I need to know which platform to be on, so I go down the steps and up the other side to look in the building. I can't see anyone. I walk out past the gate onto the street, it's in the middle of nowhere. Nothing to see except fields, so I go back to where I got off the train and sit down. If I am on the wrong platform, I could miss the connection.

Then a very noisy train whistles by, with lots and lots of containers.

I see a man in a red hat come out of the building. He must have been hiding out the back. I put my backpack on and go down the steps again to talk to him. He is at his desk by the time I get there to ask him. He says, 'Ten minutes on platform three,' which is where I was but at least I know now. I go back and a high-speed train whizzes by, the breeze from it unnerving. Then another freight train waits for its signal to go. There are no people here, but there's lots going on and it's all fascinating. I counted the containers as the train left and there were 36, that's a long train.

My hat blows off onto the railway track. In the past, I would have just let it go, but I need my hat. I know now that you can walk on train tracks. I look up and down, jump down quickly. My backpack is by the chair, not on my back, and I get my hat. It takes all of five seconds and I feel quite chuffed with myself.

My train arrives and my brief stay in Austria is over. It's a very new and modern train with digital displays that tracks every station.

Bratislava is going to be a challenge. I get in at one station and have to find my way to another. I am not doing any direct routes today, it's all over the place. I get in at Bratislava Petrzalka (needs an accent on top) station and I have to get to Bratislava Hlavna Stanica (needs an accent). I hope it's not too difficult.

Bratislava is huge. Out of the train window on the horizon, I can see rows and rows of buildings. I can see green fields, then a condensed collection of tall flats all in a huddle. There must be a reason they have left huge fields of grass and built condensed housing in flats.

I get into the station at 1.44 pm. Now I have to find my connection. I just realised I didn't show my passport to anyone and now I am in Bratislava. I have no choice but to go and speak to a human, as I have no idea how to get to Hlavna Stanica station. I find a helpful lady at the ticket office who directs me to a bus stop to get a number 93 bus. It might not be too difficult. I say thank you and walk away, only to realise that I don't know where to get a ticket, how much it is, and what currency I need. So, I go back. She is bored with me now and says that she can sell me a ticket for the bus, which is odd. I pay on my card and she raises her eyebrows. I follow her instructions to get across a very big road and find my bus stop. I have to talk to a few people to find the right stop, but they are all helpful and the piece of paper with the train station name on does help. I wouldn't be able to pronounce Hlavna Stanica. I decide to collect three words, as I am in Bratislava.

I have a ride on the 93 bendy bus across Bratislava. They are every 10 minutes and there are proper bus lanes for overtaking the traffic. I see the castle as we cross the big river. The river is very wide, and the bridge is busy with traffic. I am not disappointed that I won't be stopping here. It was somewhere I had considered, but it looks busy and noisy.

At 2.20 pm, I am on my new train. Bratislava was brief, slick, and efficient, and the people I met were very helpful. Then I change again. This is the fifth train, one more to go. We go through a tunnel and the lights go out, but it must be normal because the people continue talking.

I have been feeling a bit deaf and mute for about a week now. I can hear lots of conversations, but I can't understand a single word and I haven't been able to differentiate between Slovenian, Croatian, Hungarian, and now Slovak. When I say I am English when trying to buy tickets or food, or talk to train staff, a lot of them pull funny faces and go and find the only English-speaking person in the building. It's a bit arrogant of me to expect everyone to speak English, but I do feel out on a limb not being able to communicate. The words that come out of my mouth are falling unheard and when people talk to me, I can't understand. It's a very strange feeling. In some ways, it's isolating and lonely. I am in a bubble and I can't communicate, which feels like a disability. One of my favourite childhood books was *Helen Keller's Teacher* by Margaret Davidson. Helen was blind and deaf and I am very thankful that I am neither.

I have enjoyed all the sights out of the windows of the train, and all the exploring. To be blind or deaf or both is unimaginable. And this experience is only temporary while I am travelling through these out-of-the-way remote places.

I wonder how I will feel when I return to England. It's fate that I grew up there. All these people on the train were born in this part of the world. Did I do well or not, better or worse than these people? Or is life pretty much the same wherever you grow up? Even in England you have variations, you can grow up in St Just at the tip of Cornwall, or in London, or Scunthorpe, or anywhere in between, and you will have had a different life.

My last train of the day to Znojmo is so cute, just one carriage. A blue and white train and, just to make you feel comfortable there is an A4-sheet of paper stuck to the door window as you enter with 'Znojmo' on it.

It's a fair walk to my accommodation, about half an hour and I have done a screenshot again. It's a nice walk across a big roundabout with impressive buildings on it, then through a park and past a stadium. I go into the pub, as it has the same name as my pension: Viktoria. I am told where I'm staying is just next door, round the corner.

It's an old building with a huge door and wide concrete steps. No one answers the door, so I sneak in when a man comes out. The stone stairwell is at the front and on the landing is a door to the owners' home. It looks like a flat that they live in. I can see a kitchen ahead and rooms off the hallway. The lady is very efficient. I pay for the room and she hands me a paper bag with breakfast in it. The kitchen is being decorated or something. I am shown up the winding church-like stairs to the first floor and my room. This costs €25 a night and I get an en-suite with a toilet that has a flush. The room is big with a double bed, a lounging chair and a fridge. On the landing right outside my door is a bookshelf arrangement with a kettle and a selection of teas, which I am told I can help myself to.

Heaven.

It's a shame this is just one night. It's a huge improvement on Gyenesdiás and half the price.

I have a quick shower, a cup of very welcome tea, and go out to explore this place with the name I can't pronounce. What a gem. It's set on a hill with a river at the bottom. We are quite high up and access down doesn't look easy. It doesn't look like there's anything there if you do manage to get down but there are lots of viewpoints and stunning photo opportunities. The old town has so many interesting buildings, streets, squares, churches, and towers. It's difficult not to crick your neck looking everywhere.

The sun is low and the streets are empty, and I feel that I've seen this little place at its best. All the streets are cobbled, and I have changed into flip-flops out of my lace-up travel shoes, making it a bit difficult to walk. You couldn't wear thin heels here. I spend a few hours looking around and taking photos as there are some amazing buildings and its so pretty. I would have liked a walking tour here.

I go back to the pub next door to get a cold drink ... and they have cider. I actually clap my hands and skip. The lady must think I am crazy, especially when I ask her what currency she wants. I don't know where I am right now. I offer her the money that the other lady in the corner shop threw at me, so I must be in the Czech Republic. I buy one cider and one pink lemonade as they both look nice and I don't want a headache tomorrow from two ciders.

I go back to my room, pour out a drink in a glass and sit in the lounging chair at the table. I upload Facebook photos and message Phil. My phone won't work here, but I have Wi-Fi. I drink both drinks and eat the croissant that was in my bag for breakfast. I am not keen on them but I am hungry, again. I haven't had a meal today. The vegan thing has long gone out of the window.

Quite chuffed with my day and thinking about all the old trains I have travelled on, I am looking forward to tomorrow very much.

Znojmo to Český Krumlov
Thursday 20th August

After a solid sleep, I make myself a cup of tea from the arrangement on the landing outside my room. What a treat, so many teas to choose from and a kettle. I shower and sit with my tea in the lounging chair and work out my route to Český Krumlov. The Interrail community gives me some great help. They say it's best to get the bus as it's cheap and the bus station is closer to the centre than the rail station, so that's less walking with my backpack.

I write down my destination to communicate with the ticket lady and off I go to the train station. A little early, but I feel refreshed, and I am itching to get to Český Krumlov.

I buy my ticket, it's going to be a six-hour journey, I think, and costs about 258 Czech koruna, which I think is about £10. I buy a few snacks in a little station shop under the platforms, and then I go into the station café. The lady serving speaks as much English as I do Czech. Nada. But I manage to order a tea and sit down while she boils the kettle. This is a big train station café, with about 20 tables, so the kettle surprises me.

The tea is a cup of hot water, a tea bag on the side, and some honey or lemon syrup, just like in Croatia. But it's OK. I really only want to sit down and lap up the atmosphere.

Not being able to read or understand people's words makes you more tuned into your surroundings. Men are chatting at a table, the ladies in the kitchen are laughing. It's also quite nice not listening to other people's conversations. That part of my brain has switched off. I really am on my own and it's OK.

There is a beer mat on the table, and it throws me. This is a train station pit stop and I am surprised that they sell alcohol. But more than that, it transports me straight back to my childhood. My dad used to collect them and they bring back a lot of memories. My dad was a very clever man and worked with electronics and computers in the 70s, before most of us knew what a computer was. He used to work at Cossars in Harlow and travelled all over Europe and America fixing computers; I think. He did something electrical anyway, which must have paid well as we had a company car. Not that we went in it much as he was away or out most of the time.

He once gave me a microchip to take to school and show my teachers because it was going to change the world. He was quite right. He had an expense account that came with the job, and he travelled around Europe drinking beer and collecting beer mats. He was a member of CAMRA, the campaign for real ale. And we collected beer mats on holiday to Cornwall and Scotland as well, to add to his collection.

He was also an alcoholic. Not a string vest, special brew kind of alcoholic, but a functioning one, he rarely looked drunk but often had a temper. He drank an awful lot while out and about as well as at home from his homebrews that stank the house out.

So, this cardboard beer mat could even have been part of his collection. It's bent with the familiar wear and tear and creases that a lot of them had. The foreign logos that I don't understand, the texture of the card that is so familiar to me and gives me a very weird set of emotions. I don't want to think about my dad. I pretend I don't have one. Well, I don't. He died in 1998, alone, in a bedsit, from an alcohol-related something. Who knows?

Strangely, I saw him six months before he died but I hadn't seen him for 14 years before that, except for a brief interaction, when he came to our front door to give me my 18th birthday present. It was a bedside table that he had put together for me. I was touched by his gesture, but still filled with rage. I am ashamed to say that I took the gift and shut the door.

In the spring of 1998 we were in Boston. I went to a park to meet him which was arranged by his wife that he left my mum for, although by then they had already separated. I met my half-brother, Andrew, for the first and only time. He was about 12, I think, and it was a strange hour. My dad was late and came down a hill on a bike and was the image of my grandad with his white hair. He looked about 70 years old but was 55.

How strange, the same age as me now. That's hard to digest and process.

Anyway. I had Liam and Aidan with me, his grandchildren, but he hardly looked at them. Andrew was all over him, which is understandable, and I felt like I was intruding. The irony is that he had messed up his first family to create another and messed that one up as well.

I am a little jealous of people who have positive relationships with their dads. Pleased for them, obviously, but it's not something that I had. My dad was not the first man I ever loved, the man to set standards for a husband, although the irony is that I married a man very similar. So my dad did set a standard, but not a very high one. He wasn't a man who made me feel safe. In fact, he kicked me once, and it hurt so much that I had to take the morning off school.

When I was about 10 years old, possibly, I also got between my mum and dad when they were fighting and he knocked her glasses off and broke them. He was a very unpleasant man who I felt uncomfortable around and I was very pleased when he left.

I put the beer mat in my bag, tuck my memories away and get up. It's time to move on. I get on my train from Znojmo. I need to somehow sort out the past in my head and get all these random emotions under control.

A lady gets up and presses a red button and the train stops, just as if we were on a bus. There is no station, just a spot to get off which is very odd. The train is very bumpy, lurching sideways, and it makes me feel a little sick. We stop a lot, and I love watching the camaraderie between the staff in red hats at the stations. The fields are golden with cut hay and there are endless little towns and clusters of houses with lots of churches.

I change trains at Okrisky, a rural train station, which is very old, and tatty and full of charm. The next train to Budejovice proves a challenge to get on. It's about three feet off the ground with a ladder to use to get on. Thank goodness it also has a rail to help heave me and my backpack up. A real challenge and so Interrail.

I just finished my book, *The Authenticity Project,* which I enjoyed. It's a very clever story with equally clever characters. Back in real life, a lady comes by with a hostess trolly, like we are on a plane or in a hospital beds. It is such a cute little trolly thing, with three little baskets, the top with hot water and teas, the middle with snacks, and the bottom with cold cans. I have to buy something as it's the cutest thing ever. The lady picks up on my excitement and even lets me take a photo and helps me with the money. I get a fruit tea with the tiniest pot of lemon that I have ever seen and a packet of Oreo biscuits.

It's a nice little treat to break up a long journey and a good interlude before I start another book. It's timely and I love it.

I am glad my book is finished because the scenery is enough to entertain me, no more eternal fields but lush green trees and houses and a big pond.

I have Wi-Fi on the train, which is very unusual so I google Český Krumlov. It looks great and I think I have made the right decision to stay for three nights. I also google where to go after Český. I narrow it down to a choice between Karlovy Vary or Prague. Karlovy Vary might win as I can go to Prague easily from England.

The peace of the train is interrupted at Jindrichuv Hradec (needs all the weird acents) by an ancient couple, with not a tooth between them. They smell like ashtrays and they don't stop talking the whole time. They both have old baseball caps on, mismatched trackie bottoms and t-shirts, and an array of logos and colours. But they smile energetically at me and I can't help but like them. They could possibly be brother and sister and look between 50 and 70. It's impossible to tell. They only stay on for three stops but I can still smell them long after they have left.

At Cesky Budejovice, I get off the train and look for the bus station. I ask a lady at the bus stop outside if knows where it is. If she uses buses, she might know where the one is that I need. She points to a shopping centre that I can see on the other side of the road at the next junction. I don't see a bus station but I might as well go that way. She says to go under the underpass, well, I can't understand her words, but her fingers walk down steps and back up, and we both laugh.

When I get to the other side of the busy road I can't see the bus station, so I ask a bus driver that has pulled into a bus stop. He points up at the sky near the shopping centre. I follow his directions to the entrance of the shopping centre. I look up and there's the bus stop on top of the shops. I wasn't expecting that, but what a great idea.

I go up the escalators inside the shopping centre, to the top, and find my bus. It's all very organised and easy to follow. I have half an hour to wait, so I go back down to the shops and find myself queuing at a Chinese takeaway for veggie noodles. I love veggie noodles and this seems a great opportunity to get some. I don't think I have ever bought noodles in a shopping precinct before. It's not something Cornwall offers.

I eat them upstairs where the buses are, leaning against a wall while I wait for my bus. They are hot and delicious and very satisfying. I put them away when the bus arrives and get on. I am eager now. I can't wait to see if Český Krumlov is as lovely as I hope it is. I have been thinking about going there since I was researching in the lockdown.

Stepping off the bus at Český Krumlov, when I reach my destination, I am very excited. This is my home for three nights. It's been a while since I stayed anywhere for three nights, so that alone is good. I follow the screenshot on my phone down some steps and across a road. I then turn right and go over a bridge and onto cobblestones. I can feel by the buildings and the atmosphere that the whole place is steeped in history.

There are terracotta rooftops and towers to the right, as well as big buildings with huge stone doorways and arched wooden doors. I go past a posh-looking hotel where the front has unusual decoration and a scalloped top. Then I pass a dusky pink building with an ornate roof and raised decoration on the walls.

I can't take it all in, it's full of character and charm, and I can't wait to explore. I pass a huge church, tucked away, but huge and tall. Everything is built up and densely packed together, with narrow roads and tall buildings. It reminds me a little of Venice in a strange way, although it's quite different. I end up in a big square, turn left down a tiny street, and find my hotel: Krcinuv Dum. I have struck gold and can't help smiling. I had forgotten which hotel I booked as I had spent so long looking at them. I can't believe I will be staying here. This must be the 14th century one, it's full of character with beige bricks and lots of red window frames. There are tables and chairs out the front, a little pavement café. It's perfect.

When I check in, the lady walks me up an ancient, winding concrete staircase and to my room, which is beautiful. It's absolutely the icing on the cake. It has a big wooden bed, two large windows looking down on the street, framed with huge, heavy pink velvet curtains. The floor is wooden with an old rug on it. I love it.

I ask her for a kettle as the last two days without tea were painful. She goes off and returns with a kettle. Three days with my own kettle. Bliss.

As I am here for three whole days, I hang my clothes up in the big wooden wardrobe. It's the first time I have hung up my clothes on this trip, and this wardrobe is begging to be filled. Not that I can fill it with my handful of things but it makes me feel more settled. This feels like a holiday within my holiday.

I make myself green tea and jump in the shower while it brews a bit. The shower has two shower heads which confuses me, I do find showers a struggle, too many buttons and now two showers.

After the shower I drag the chair from the desk over to the window. I have a very deep window ledge, as this is a 14th century building and the walls are so thick. Out of my window below is a sort of triangle, not a square. It's where the buildings curve on an angle, and the street follows, creating this little courtyard effect with pavement seating from two restaurants on the right-hand side, and the ones from this hotel underneath me. I sit back, drink my tea and have a few biscuits that I bought in a shop at the train station at Znojmo, and watch the world go by.

Later, fully refreshed and happy I go out to explore. Everywhere you look are colourful, proud, ornate buildings and then I come out of the small lanes and into the open across a wooden bridge. A river runs underneath it and ahead is a huge castle,

The natural bend of the river has formed Český Krumlov. The buildings are nestled in what looks and feels like an island because there is water on nearly all sides, and you cross a bridge to get in. I stand on the bridge and look up at a castle. There's a pretty tower to my right and a dam on the river. There is so much to take in. People are bobbing by in rafts on the river. This place is unique and I love it. I go over to the castle, but it's big and I can't find an entrance or any information. So, the first thing I need to do is find the tourist information office as the hotel lady suggested.

It's very busy in the tourist office, with people and leaflets, so there's lots to do here. After reading everything I could find in English, I decide to buy the Gold Card which will get me into a lot of the tourist things.

I can't stop taking photos. I walk back to the bus station as it's a bit higher and has a great view of Český Krumlov. There's a petrol station there too, so I pop in and buy a bottle of Orange Fanta and a bottle of wine, and some crisps. I am not quite sure what I have spent but I don't really care. I head back to my room and park myself in the window again. The deep, wooden window ledge is like a desk. I have my drink and crisps and I get out all the touristy bits of paper to study so I can decide what to do tomorrow.

I also book two nights at Karlovy Vary, as I don't want to have to think about where to go next while I am enjoying myself here. Usually I enjoy all the planning but this place is sensory overload and I want to enjoy all of it without any distraction.

I have a glass of wine and eat some cold noodles which are surprisingly nice, then I chill for a bit before bed.

Český Krumlov
Friday 21st August

I start my day with a luxurious buffet breakfast in a beautiful 14th century ground floor room overlooking the triangle. There is lots of fruit, proper tasty apple juice, toast, and a selection of jams. It is just what I needed. I chill for ages, enjoying it all.

Then I go over to the main big square for my walking tour and look for a man with a large yellow umbrella. I am the first one there, which is very awkward. He has perfect English and is chatty, which I assume is a natural trait for a job like this. He talks about cancelling, which I am happy about. Well, not happy, but I don't want it to be just the two of us. That's weird. These are free walking tours, but everyone chips in and if it's only me, I would feel obliged to pay a lot more. Then a couple turns up, and he decides three is OK, so off we go.

He talks about the big square we are in now and how it was once filled with tanks and even gets a photo out on his phone to show us. It's difficult to believe because we are on what feels like an island, and whilst this square is plenty big enough, the lanes leading to it are very narrow and winding.

We walk round to my hotel and stand in front of it and he tells us the history. My hotel is a landmark on his tour, what a surprise. He tells us about the special artwork on the outside of the building. I don't mention that there's my room just there with my windowsill full of leaflets. I don't know why I don't tell them, maybe because I am a bit shy. Or maybe because there are only three of us and they will think I am rich, when it actually was a very reasonable price. I just choose not to tell them and we move on, with me smiling.

We walk over the bridge to the castle, which is great because now I know how to get up there. He takes us to the courtyard, and he brings it alive and fills us with images of the past, with animals being bought and sold. It's very interesting. We walk to the Baroque theatre and learn all about that, then follow the passageway from the castle up to the gardens.

After an hour and a half, we part company. I decide to give him €5.00 which is exactly what I planned to give him.

The next thing to do is get to the top of the tower, which is included in my Gold Card and I bet the views are great. My card doesn't work and the lady who sold it to me said it would, so I sneak in with a family, muttering and jesting that it's not working. They don't seem to mind. The 360-degrees views from the tiny walk around at the top is stunning. From here, I can see the way the river wraps itself around in a loop, forming the island with all the densely packed buildings.

I am blessed with gorgeous weather and the water below twinkles. The sun is shining, boats are in the river, tiny people are crossing the bridge down below and I absolutely love this place. I walk around for a few times, taking lots of photos and getting in people's way, it's very tiny. I get my selfie stick out. I am getting much less self-conscious now. I wish I had done this years ago. If I had gone through life with fewer inhibitions, it might have been quite a different life altogether. I might have stood up to people instead of giving in, I might have travelled more, made better decisions. Just been a bit more confident.

That was fun. I go down to the castle tourist information to get a ticket for the castle. It's not included in the Gold Card so I got stung there. Only the tower and the museum. I buy a ticket anyway. They are all organised according to language, so I need the English one at 2.30 pm. I have spent a lot of money here, more than anywhere so far, but I want to go in the castle, so I have to pay.

I have a bit of time to spare and go back to the hotel, have a cup of tea and some biscuits, which has probably saved me some money, and watch the people in the triangle again.

When it's time, I wander back over to the castle for my tour. We have to wait outside a door in the castle grounds, which is up a very steep slope and through a courtyard area to a big door. A lady in a long dress comes out at exactly 2.30 pm, which is a bit unnerving as I didn't know if I was in the right place. We are immediately told not to take any photos, which I think is a bit mean.

The lady is a good host; she tells us of all the families who have lived in the castle, of accidental shootings and change of ownership. I didn't know that, in the past, people slept in beds sitting upright, which is why they are all very short beds, or that the rugs on the walls were to keep the rooms warm. So, I am learning a lot, but it is simply lovely to wander around the castle in the wonderful rooms and learn something new. History has never been interesting to me and I had very, very few history lessons at my school, Passmores Comprehensive school in Harlow where I grew up. But I do like people history.

The last room that we go into is a real treat. It's called the Masquerade Hall. It's a large room, like a small ballroom, with the most stunning artwork on the walls and a big empty floor. There are big murals of people having fun, some aristocratic and some poor people, so even though the room is empty, it feels full. There are paintings of balconies filled with people who look like a lot of fun, colourful with big expressions. They are all dressed in flouncy clothes, including jesters, and all of them appear to be having a great time at a ball.

It's very special and the artist, who apparently painted the whole room on his own, was clearly amazing and talented at capturing all the characters. The guide tells us that some of the faces are looking at people on the opposite wall and the humour is everywhere to see. I could easily stay in this one room all afternoon.

I step out of the castle, buzzing. As I walk back across the courtyard, it feels different. I look up at the windows in the courtyard and see the window that I looked out off from inside down to where I am now. It was a good decision to go into the castle.

Knowing I have some time, I go over to the monastery before it shuts. It's included in my Gold Card. Unfortunately, it isn't very interesting. Which is a shame. It is lovely and quiet, with big white walls, and lots of things to read. But not great. I feel like I am in a boring museum rather than a monastery. But never mind, time for food. I know exactly where I want to sit and eat my dinner: down by the river, on the edge of the water by the bridge. Now I have to find a restaurant that I like the look of with suitable food. If there is no food, I will have a drink at least.

From the bridge, I see a row of outdoor seats right on the edge of the river. I'm not sure how to get there. I leave the bridge, turn left up the first alleyway, and find a discreet entrance with a menu displayed outside. I can't see anything on the menu that I fancy, but I go in anyway. I walk down through a dark entrance and then out to a seating area next to the river. Perfect. Except there aren't any free seats next to the water. I can see another restaurant next door, so I go out, find the next entrance and the exact seat where I want to sit next to the water. I pick up the menu and can't believe my eyes: veggie/vegan. Thank goodness they had no seats next door.

A happy smiley owner comes to make sure I have a menu. I struggle to choose because there are a few things that I want.

I decide on roasted mushrooms, and the owner offers me rice or potatoes with it. I opt for the boiled potatoes. This could go either way, delicious or disgusting. But when it arrives, it is amazing and I want the recipe. He declines.

It's really delicious, the mushrooms must have been roasting away with onions and peppers all day, and the flavour is intense with lots of scrummy sauce. The potatoes are perfectly cooked. There is also a salad of fresh young spinach and cucumber and tomato, all complementing each other. For such a humble meal, it is utterly delicious. I want to try to re-create this at home.

The setting is perfect; the river is busy with people floating by and the sun is shining. It has a different feel to the rest of Český Krumlov, as it's by the river. I want to stay in this beautiful spot a bit longer, so I order a homemade lemonade. The owner brings me a homemade orangeade, but it's delicious. Fresh and tasty, with bits of orange in every mouthful.

I sit back and chill. It's been a full, but fun day, so much for chilling for three days. I watch people drifting by in all sorts of rubber rings, blow up canoes for two and larger family-size boats. A very noisy boat goes by with people laughing and having fun, possibly a little merry from alcohol. They keep crashing into the sides of the bank. They are followed by other boats, full of more serious people, who know how to move the boat about.

Children are sitting on the bank of the river and an elderly man is trying to swim, but the water isn't deep enough. There are some very old houses and to my left, a beautiful white and grey church tower, which looks like it's been converted into accommodation. The walking tour man said the organ from inside is now in the other big church.

The restaurant is called Laibon, and it said on the wall that it was established in 1535. I love Český Krumlov. I feel totally at peace. I am definitely living in the moment. I have so many memories of all the places I have been to: Morzine, Geneva,

Montreux, Switzerland, Venice, Ljubljana. It's all been amazing, but right now, I am here. Really here.

I can't believe that I have been so lucky with the weather and the choice of places that I have been to and I am still not finished. But, right now, I am enjoying this delicious drink and watching the people drifting by, and thinking how incredibly lucky I am.

By now, it's just after 6.00 pm and I am not quite ready to go back to the hotel. It's warm and still sunny enough to wear sunglasses. So, I walk back over the bridge towards the castle, but this time turn left and walk along the river on the opposite side, looking back at the 'island'. It's so lovely that I keep on walking, following the river. I find a park with lots of willow trees and think of Phil as he has a willow in his front garden. I get a really good look at the church as it backs onto the river.

I stumble across a small shop, which would be easy to miss, as it's long and narrow and looks nothing like a supermarket from the outside. I spot a donut and pop it in a bakery bag. It will be perfect with a cup of tea back at the hotel.

I get back to my room and make myself comfy. I open the big double windows, and just below me, next to the pizza place, is live entertainment.

I think about my journey home and try to get a rough plan together, so that I can work out how many Interrail days I need to get home. There are so many decisions and timetables. Ciara has texted me and said that she has booked her ticket to Frankfurt and we plan to meet in Mainz, so I book a hotel there. I can't believe I am going to see Ciara as well on my trip. It's a bit random.

The donut and tea are delicious, and the music is very welcome. I am forever thankful for this lovely room. I feel like I am outside, but I have all my comforts around me.

The musicians swap just as the sun goes down, and this new people's music is wonderful. I can't understand a word, but the lady's voice is beautiful, the music, violins and shakers are so atmospheric and very Czech. I love it so much that I film some of it. Then I pour out a glass of wine from the bottle I bought yesterday which was in the mini-fridge, lean back and enjoy it.

The music gets even better as it gets dark and the little triangle below is lit by lights in the restaurant. Everyone in the pizza place is listening and swaying. I have my dressing gown on, chilling with my feet up on the windowsill. Her beautiful voice echoes around the buildings and it's so intimate. People start to join in, and a church bell even rings. It's such a treat, and it almost brings a tear to my eye. I film more of it, to try and capture the atmosphere. There is appreciative clapping at the ending. Another highlight of my trip.

Saturday 22ndAugust

Today I need to get a ticket to view the inside of the Baroque theatre. The man told us a bit of history about it on the walking tour yesterday and then Daisy, my niece, messaged me last night, saying that although she hasn't been here, she knows it's one of only four surviving Baroque theatres and it's the best. I know nothing about theatre but Daisy does, as she has a degree in Theatre Management. So, on her behalf and because I am here and because why not, I decide I will go and check it out. But I have to get to the front of the queue to get a ticket early as they sold out yesterday. Plus, the English tour starts at 10.00 am.

So, I am at breakfast at 8.15 am. It's busier this morning, and the food is just as good. Afterwards, I go and buy my ticket. This is a very expensive place if you want to get into all the buildings. I have a bit of time free time before the tour starts, so I take a walk up to the walled garden. It is delightful, just what you would expect, formal straight lines and trees and fountains.

Then it's time to go into the theatre. It's full of history and simply stunning. It's one of only two remaining in Europe. It's so beautiful, every wall is covered in paintings, as well as the ceilings and the balcony. There is also a walkway from the castle directly into the theatre that can be seen from outside. It's a corridor that connects the castle to the theatre, so that the occupants and guests of the castle didn't have to go outside. It comes in at the upper level and must have been a very impressive entrance.

The stage scenery can be changed in seconds due to the elaborate machinery under the stage and our tour guide takes us down under the stage so that we can see. There is wood everywhere, and, long ago, the theatre would have been lit with candles, which is why there are only a couple left. It's a very precious part of history.

Daisy is going to love it when she gets here.

I squeeze in an art museum trip on the way back to the hotel but it doesn't interest me much. So, I go to my room and have a nice cup of tea and a donut that I brazenly stole from breakfast this morning. It has a yummy apricot filling.

Afterwards, I go to another museum included in my Gold Card. The lovely ladies offer me a locker for my bag because it looks heavy. They should see my other bag – this is just my small day bag. They look surprised that I take it with me. The museum is a bit dull, well, to me it is, probably not everyone. But I am keen to see the ceramic model of the village on the top floor. It's worth the walk up as it's stunning, accurate replica of Český Krumlov. A work of art. I walk around and round, looking at places I recognise. I find my hotel and the triangle, the big church, which I can see in detail from this angle, and even where I ate my dinner last night. I notice details I never took in while I was walking on the ground and at the top of the tower in real life. The castle, the walkway to the theatre, and the walled garden are there. It's charming and beautifully made.

As I am close to the entrance and the bridge, I walk over to the bus station to sort out my ticket for tomorrow. I can't believe I am leaving. It's whizzed by. When I looked I couldn't find any timetables online, so I am going to look at the actual bus station. Unfortunately, no one there speaks English, not one person. None of the people waiting for buses, and none of the bus drivers. I feel like an alien.

So, I walk back and find myself at a different spot on the river, where people get on and off the rafts or boats rather than drift by. I sit down and smell chips, thinking that's a great idea. It's a sort of takeaway with benches by the river under the trees. Before you know it, I have ordered a portion of chips and a half of cider. Who cares, I am on holiday and it was only 90 koruna, which I don't think is very much.

I watch the rafts and boats whizz by for about an hour. There are lots of people going round in circles, getting nowhere. And even a dog on one raft who seems to be enjoying himself. Plus an inflatable unicorn.

I then go to three different mini markets in search of donuts and fail. Biscuits and tea it is then, back at the hotel. I try to book a Eurostar ticket home, but every time I put it in my basket, it says it's not available. After a frustrating hour, I give up.

Getting hungry, I go back to the same restaurant as before, thinking of getting the burger but, in the end, I go with the mushrooms again as I enjoyed them so much yesterday. The weather is not as good as yesterday; I can feel a breeze and possibly rain coming. There are still people whizzing by on the water, some very wobbly people in the rafts, looking like they are going to end up in the water. But at least they all look like they are having fun.

Booking my Eurostar means my holiday is coming to an end. In some ways, I can't wait to get home but I am also enjoying the freedom so much that I want to carry on. I haven't been free much in my life, like many other people. I have always restrained by situations, people, circumstances, and probably myself. I am not very good at letting my hair down. I absolutely hate being the centre of attention. In fact, I don't like people looking at me at all. I don't buy raffle tickets because walking across a room to go and get my prize fills me with dread.

This has been a very selfish trip. It's been exactly what I wanted it to be, and I have done exactly what I wanted to do; it's been a revelation. No one has suffered because I was selfish. It doesn't have to be a choice between my happiness or someone else's. We can all be happy. I need to be a bit more selfish from now on. Not so that it hurts others, but do a bit more of what makes me happy. It is my life, after all. I dedicated myself to my children as they were growing and took the job as 'Mum' very responsibly. Despite its many challenges, I thoroughly enjoyed it and loved seeing my three grow into wonderful adults and see Jamie thrive as well. It's been very rewarding, but now it's time to learn how to be more selfish. To put me first if I want to. I am not sure that I can break the habit, or change the way that I live my life, but I am going to try.

I feel that I have grown as a person on this trip. I can take selfies now without feeling as silly as I did the first few times in Venice. I can talk to strangers much more easily than I used to. I jump on and off of trains, not always being sure that I am on the right one. I have felt such freedom that I can't put into words.

Imagine if I had done this in my late teens. I wonder if I would have been a more confident person and taken up more opportunities, like university, which sounded far too social and scary to me. I could have trained as a teacher, which is what I wanted to be all through my childhood, but the thought of going to university put me off. Or being a nurse, which I would have been good at. I started on a course when I was 23 years old, but I bailed on my course because they kept making us do talks in front of the class. I hated it and I had a panic attack and nearly passed out instead of doing my talk. I left the course, which was a really bad decision.

I have stayed in jobs for too long for fear of handing in my notice, stayed in relationships too long for fear of upsetting people. I have been a bit weak, and it was probably all rooted in a lack of confidence. My friends on Facebook think I am brave for doing this trip, which is strange as I know a lot of them appear to me, far more confident and equipped to do this trip than I am.

I don't know where you get your confidence from. Why are some people confident and others not? Is it from your childhood? Your parents? School teachers? Or maybe we are born confident but have it knocked out of us by life and situations. Or maybe we are just all different and comparing ourselves to others is the worst thing you can do. We are all unique. Some are nurtured better as children by loving parents. Some don't have parents at all and are raised by others. But you hear of people from difficult backgrounds achieving great things and people from good backgrounds who achieve nothing.

I didn't have anyone by my side guiding me. My dad left, although my mum was there for me, she listened to me a lot. I even sat on the edge of her bath when she probably wanted some alone time, but she never turned me away. She provided us with a stable and secure life. But all despite this, she didn't actively guide me, not that I can remember. Maybe I have forgotten. Maybe when you are young, you don't listen to advice, thinking you know it all.

I feel that I failed myself and my full potential. The teachers could have guided me. I was in the sixth form at school, so all the teachers knew me, but I can't remember one conversation about my future with any teacher. Not one person sat me down and told me the options I had. I blindly followed a path that I don't remember taking for myself. I didn't fully understand what the options were and blundered my way through, making bad decisions.

One thing I have started to understand on this trip is that my life hasn't been perfect. But whose has? What I need to do now is move forwards, file it all away as part of what made me who I am and appreciate what I have now. Which is an awful lot.

I am ready to return to Cornwall and pick up my life again. I want to travel more. Go on city breaks to Prague, Budapest, Barcelona. Go to Croatia, Plitvice Lakes and down to Montenegro. I think I will do that now, without the hesitation and the what-ifs.

I pay my bill and reluctantly tear myself away from the river's edge and this restaurant. I have explored everywhere that I wanted to. I have been really lucky with the weather and decide it's time to head back to the hotel. I have managed to find a bus timetable, so at least I have some times now.

Back at the hotel in my window seat, I pour out the rest of the wine. One last glass for my last night here. There isn't any music this evening, it must be a Friday night event. The triangle below is quiet. But that's nice too. It's been a pretty full-on trip to Český Krumlov.

I get off to sleep quickly, probably because I walked five and a half miles today, but I am awoken dead on 3.00 am by two drunk men downstairs in the triangle. Their drunk voices echo around the buildings. I freeze, while my brain processes it. I can't understand a word, but I know that they are slurring. One of them is far drunker than the other with almost animal grunts coming from him, as he is past forming proper sentences.

I can feel every heartbeat in my chest and remind myself over and over that this has nothing to do with me. They won't be coming anywhere near me and I am safe. I lie still in bed, in the dark, listening for clues.

There's a crash, a heavy sound but no furniture noises. I am guessing that one of them has fallen over. It goes quiet for a bit.

I am wide awake now, unfortunately. I jump out of bed, my body on high alert, and I look out of the window cautiously. I see a lady putting bags in her car. She must be checking out, which is a strange time, perhaps she has a flight to catch or something. She looks over at the men nervously, so I know they are in the hotel doorway underneath my window. She drives off and the triangle below is again dark and quiet.

My teeth are clenched and my body is frozen. My pulse races. My body has remembered all those times when it really was in danger and didn't know what was going to happen next. Being woken by a drunk, volatile man is horrible. My body right now is confused, my brain can't process that I am safe, even if I am trying to reassure myself.

It's been quiet for a while now. They are probably unconscious on the floor.

I try to get back to sleep but keep looking at the clock. It's 3.47 am. The men are moving about and trying to talk to each other. The knot in my stomach is so big that I can't get comfortable. The church bells ring twice at four o'clock. Why? It's the middle of the night. The silence continues and I fall asleep.

Český Krumlov to Karlovy Vary
Sunday 23rd August

My alarm wakes me at 7.20 am and I don't feel that refreshed, but I get up anyway. I need to be at breakfast with my bag at 8.00 am so that I can leave immediately after and get the 8.55 am bus.

The reception should be manned at 8.00 am. It has a big iron door with a curved top that I can see through into a small room with a curved ceiling. This is, after all, a 14th century building. On the gate is a note saying reception opens at 8.00 am. I ask the ladies looking after the buffet where the receptionist is, and apparently, she has children to take care of and won't be in until 9.00 am, is that OK? I explain that it's not really OK as I need to pay and leave by 8.30 am. So, one lady kindly phones her and we arrange for her to bill me.

My third breakfast here is delicious and I take some food for my lunch, then pick up my rucksack and leave.

Walking back over the stone bridge, I know I did everything possible to do in Český Krumlov in the time I've had, and thoroughly enjoyed all of it.

A young Czech girl behind me calls out and asks me if I know the way to the bus station. We walk together and she tells me she has been dancing all night with friends. We wait at the bus stop together and she laughs that I can't pronounce Cesky

Budejovice, which is the bus stop that I need to buy a ticket for. She tries to teach me, which is amusing. It doesn't feel like I would ever be able to get the pronunciation right. When the bus arrives, she gets on first and I ask her if she will talk to the bus driver for me and she says no; I must try. She laughs with the driver, retelling the story of me not being able to pronounce it, which is funny. I follow her onto the bus and try to say Cesky Budejovice, even though he now knows where I am going. It's all very amusing and friendly. The bus driver replies to me with a big, bright 'Super!' which is so out of context, it makes me laugh.

I sit opposite the young girl on the bus and I ask her what 'thank you' is in Czech. When she tells me, It's impossible for me to say, I would have to take all my teeth out and put them back in a different order to say that. She laughs. She is a bit of light relief after last night and it's lovely to mingle with the local people. She gets off on the outskirts of Cesky Budejovice in a pretty village with a green.

I am a little annoyed that I didn't have unbroken sleep last night. I paid a lot of money for the hotel and loved the place. I didn't want to be woken by drunk men outside. But it's not the hotel's fault, it's just one of those things. Anyone would have been woken by them. It's normal for me to react irrationally to situations like last night, and I just have to move on.

Sometimes, I have bad dreams for no apparent reason. And sometimes, if triggered, my mind has a box set of horror films stored away with labels on. All the bad experiences that I have been through are filed away neatly. And sometimes, if triggered by something, my mind decides to play them randomly without my consent or control, not in any particular order, just a bad collection of random memories.

Sometimes when you hear a song or smell something, or even taste something, it takes you to a happy place. It's similar to that.

But in those situations you are in control, you can choose to put the memory aside, or explore it a bit more and it's all good, fluffy, happy memories.

Mine is not a box set of happy memories. They are awful, terrible times and they play one after the other without me being able to switch them off. I feel all the horrible feelings and emotions of fear and panic that went with the real situations at the time they happened the first time.

I met and married my husband within about nine months, and we had children immediately, just as we both wanted. But I felt like a fish who had been caught on the end of a barbed fishing hook. And getting off that hook would probably had a worse outcome and be more painful than staying still.

From the moment I met him, I felt stuck. I knew it wasn't the right choice, but I also felt like I couldn't get out of it either. He was asked to move out of the flat where we were living, due to his behaviour. I should have ended it that day, but we found somewhere else to live. It was a bad choice and probably the biggest regret in my life. I stopped seeing my friends, as they didn't like him and we were living together full time almost immediately. It's like the life I had before stopped. A huge part of me was excited to get married and have children, and another part of me felt trapped. And it went from bad to worse, and worse again during those first few years. I don't have good memories of the boys when they were very small. They were very bleak, lonely, pretty awful times.

I had postnatal depression with Aidan, which the midwife wrote in my red book, but didn't do anything about it. Luckily, that wouldn't happen today, but it happened to me. People used to say that I wasn't coping because I had two children very close together. But the fact was, I had a husband who often didn't come home at night and wasn't supportive if he was home.

So, two very young children and postnatal depression, and very little support.

The bus goes up the ramp to the top of the shopping precinct and I am back in Cesky Budejovice where I was a couple of days ago, but I feel richer for the wonderful experience that was Český Krumlov. It is a very special place, and I am thrilled that I made the effort to get there. Even my experience last night and my brain wandering a bit today are not going to spoil my trip.

I know the way back to the train station: through the underpass that goes beneath the main road. I get one train to Plzen, then change onto a high-speed train to Cheb. It's 20 minutes late and packed solid with people squashed into the middle aisle. And I am one of two people wearing their mask as it's not compulsory in the Czech Republic.

It's a strange, slim train, with one seat on the left aisles and two on the right. I have not seen one like it before. It feels like an old people's convention; 90% of people here look 70 or 80 years old, and they all seem to know each other. There are lots and lots of suitcases and it's a real squash. It's an hour-and-a-half journey and I can't read my Kindle standing up, but I do scan Facebook to keep me entertained as there is free Wi-Fi.

Ciara has messaged me to say that she has landed in Germany. Calvin picked her up, and they have gone to eat in Mainz. Ciara met Calvin when she was about 13 years old, at an ice cream stand. She was on a school trip to Germany and Ciara and Gracie got chatting to him with the help of their German teacher, Mrs Rundle, as they didn't know much German. Then they kept in touch. Ciara is now 22, and she has not seen him or hardly spoken to him in all those years, and now she is going to stay at his house. It's a little random.

But in Ciara's own words, you've got to 'risk it for a biscuit' which, translated, I think means if you don't take risks you don't get anywhere or experience anything. I can hardly comment, wandering around Europe on my own, but staying alone at a man's house when you don't know much about him sounds like a huge risk to me. Strangely, I am not that worried. I trust her judgement and instinct.

I only picked Mainz as it's at the bottom of the Rhine, for no other reason, and it turns out that Ciara's German friend has an office in Mainz. Sometimes these things spook me out. All those probabilities and coincidences.

I use the free Wi-Fi to look up what to do in Karlovy Vary, but it's not easy, as it feels like the entire train wants to pass me to go to the loo. A carriage full of weak bladders. They all shuffle past while I lean over the poor person sitting on the chair below me. There's no social distancing, no masks, no care about any virus here.

I arrive at Cheb but because the train was late, I have missed my connection to Karlovy Vary and I think about getting a bus. It's a big, organised bus station in a half-circle, all numbered, but I can't see any timetables and the office in the middle of the circle is shut. I ask a few people and get directed to a bus stop, where I talk to a lovely lady who speaks good English. She tells me that we have to wait for all the people with tickets to get on to see if there's any room left. If there is, we can get on, which seems fair. In the end, we are very lucky and it turns out that the driver's ticket machine is broken so he just tells us to get on. The lady gets off one stop before me and tells me that my stop is next, which is lovely of her.

I know there's going to be a 35-minute walk to my hotel and I think about getting a taxi. I prefer to walk to get a feel for the place and it looks like I just need to follow the river. Plus, I can't see a taxi anywhere.

I walk out of the station and don't have a clue where to go. After a bit of dithering, I spot the town centre which feels like the right direction. I do have a screenshot of the journey, but because it's a long walk, it's not very detailed. I walk up through the town centre and find the river. My map isn't making much sense, but I carry on. It's an interesting place, full of impressive, tall regency buildings that line the river. I read that it was a very wealthy spa town once, and you can picture that from these lovely hotels, all painted in delicate pastel colours. I carry on walking. It's taking a long time to get to the area where I think the hotel is and it starts to drizzle. My bag is getting heavier now. I know the hotel is near the big church and I can see that; you can't miss it. But I don't know where to go, so I pop into another hotel. They will know.

Unfortunately, they don't, or they don't want to tell me. I hover in the doorway, out of the rain, trying to read my map, and the gruff lady from reception comes over and shuts the door which isn't very friendly.

I walk round the back of the church up a steep hill. It's hard work and when I get there, I can't find any hotels. I am tired now and a bit damp from the drizzle. I come back down another way. The hotel doesn't seem to be up there and find myself in a private area, maybe someone's garden.

I spot another hotel reception and they very kindly tell me how to get to the hotel: back up the hill but turn a different way. Finally, there is the hotel. Thank goodness. 'Jean de Caro' is written on the side of the hotel. Two miles, and an hour's walk up and down hills and I am here.

It's lovely here, I can't believe the view from the outside. The entrance is at the front of the hotel and there is a narrow strip of terrace, next to a fence with a view across the town. You can see all of the river, left and right. No wonder I couldn't find it, it's tucked away halfway up a hill, but the views are amazing. I go inside. I only have a budget room, but it's OK. I can sit on these little chairs by the railings with the umbrellas and have a drink later. I am looking forward to that already.

When I use my key to my room and step inside, I am blown away. It's a very average but perfectly nice room, but the view out of the window is something else. It's the same as downstairs, but even better at this height. I didn't pay for a good view; I think I have been upgraded. The room has two windows with two mini balconies. I just can't believe it. I am thrilled.

I can't have a kettle, I have already asked, but I can ask for hot water at the bar. 'Bar' is a bit of an exaggeration. It's a curved bit of wood in the corner of the reception, but there is a kettle. So, I put my bag down and go straight down and get a cup of tea. I am given a cup, so drop my loose green tea in the bottom and the lady pours hot water on it. I get the lift back to my room, where I drag the chair over to the window and open it so I can enjoy the view.

This trip is quite unbelievable. This morning I was in Český Krumlov, now I am in a different style hotel in Karlovy Vary, in the top left-hand corner of the Czech Republic, right near Germany. I am so lucky.

I drink my tea and get ready to go out and explore. The lady at reception suggests that I go and sample the hot spring water. I saw something about that on my way through town, people walking around, drinking out of strange little cups with long spouts. She says I could buy one as a souvenir or she could lend me a cup. I don't need a funny cup with a long spout, so I take the free cup.

The first thing I see is a hot spring coming straight out of the river. I can see the steam coming off it and the wall has turned a strange orange colour. To the left of the hotel is a big geyser, throwing water up into the air at intervals. I wander down the side of the river, back the way I came from the train station, and cross over one of the bridges to a spot where there is an ornate bandstand. In the middle people are filling up their funny cups and sitting down to drink it. I suss it out for a bit, as it's a little strange and unusual. But I am curious. I must have a go at this and taste this spring water, which apparently has healing properties.

I pluck up the courage to take my hotel-branded teacup over to the fountain and fill it up, then take a sip. It's hot, and sort of salty, very odd. It's not that pleasant, but I force myself to drink a bit more as it seems rude to throw it away. It's difficult to drink. I put the cup back in my bag. I won't be drinking that again.

I am a little hungry, as I only had a banana roll on the way, and now I need something else. For the second time on this trip, I opt for McDonald's chips. There are loads of restaurants and cafes, but I don't want to pay for a proper meal as I need to watch my pennies a bit after Český Krumlov. I also don't want to sit in a restaurant on my own. Chips are fast and efficient.

On the way back, I find a tiny corner shop and buy a Frisco cider, a bag of crisps before going back to my room. I watch the sun go down from my balcony. The sky is pink across the top of the buildings. I simply can't believe how lucky I am.

Karlovy Vary
Monday 24th August

I slept very well and woke to the sound of a geyser outside. I am lucky enough to have woken to the sound of waves before as I have had many short breaks by the sea and lots of camping trips to Pentewen Sands, which is a campsite on the beach. I have never woken to a thermal spring gushing out of the ground into a big fountain. It has a very similar, rhythmic pattern to the ocean. It's a gush rather than a wave crashing, but still a pleasant noise. I lie listening to it for a while. I am feeling quite relaxed today. Český Krumlov was a bit hectic, in a good way, but Karlovy Vary is completely different.

The breakfast is good: buffet style and a very nice spread in a very typical hotel breakfast room. I am not in any hurry today so I relax and have four cups of green tea and lots of watermelon, fresh pineapple, orange juice, rolls, and a piece of sweet bread with jam on.

Afterwards, I go back to my room and stay there. I don't really need to go out as I can see everything from my room. Lying on my bed, I can see the pretty houses opposite on the other side of the river, or I could sit on the balcony. Why would I want to be anywhere else with a view like that? My legs could do with a rest. I walked over 10 miles in Český Krumlov. I have been walking anything from four to 11 miles a day for over three weeks, as there has been so much to explore. I make a decision, or maybe my body decides for me, to have an 'in' day. I am going to spend the day in my room and I am very happy about that.

The rules on the pandemic change frequently and, despite me having bought a Eurostar reservation, which took me hours to book and cost £30, I will now have to fly home from Germany. I am gutted as I was looking forward to going to Lille and exploring that bit of France, and going back on the Eurostar, like a complete circle. But if I do that, I have to quarantine for 14 days. I am not sure where you are supposed to quarantine. Surely doing that at home with Phil working and Maria going back to college is not practical. I would need to use the bathroom and kitchen, so if I was infectious, I would pass it on. Anyway, to avoid that, I will fly home.

So, the plan is to get a test as soon as I can in England and go to a hotel until it's safe to return to the house. It's morally the right thing to do. I will book a flight when I see Ciara in Mainz. It's not ideal, but it's not bad either. How can any of this be bad? I am exceptionally lucky.

I set my chair up on the mini balcony again. It's so small I can only get the front two legs of the chair out there. It's a half-circle balcony and I can see the whole of Karlovy Vary. I wouldn't say it's pretty, but it is impressive and sort of regal. I relax and read my Kindle, stopping every so often to look at the view. There is no hurry today. The buildings opposite are mainly hotels. They are all different pastel colours, pale pink, pale blue, beige, pale yellow, pale green, sand. They are all terraced together, and on the hill opposite, I can count 14 floors. They are framed by trees and if I look carefully up on the hill, I can see the funicular up to Diana Tower where you can get a great view. I was thinking of doing that, but I am being a bit mean with my money and I can't believe the view is any better than I have here. Maybe it is, but I don't have the energy or inclination today.

I drink the orange juice that I was given for breakfast in Znojmo and eat a peach from my first day's breakfast in Český Krumlov, which is now perfectly ripe and delicious.

As a bit of a break, I decide to take some photos of the view and then I take some more selfies. I have fun, and get some half-decent photos of me, the best I am going to manage with this face. But I keep telling myself that getting old is a privilege and we all know people who died much younger than they should have, so how can we complain about getting old and looking old? It's perfectly normal.

I need another cup of tea and go down to reception for more hot water and bring it back to my balcony to drink.

Then at 2.30 pm, I decide to go for a little stroll. I will need to find some food of some sort. I could eat in the hotel, but it looked a bit formal and a bit of fresh air will be good.

I walk up by the river again, well there's nowhere else to walk. I could go the river one way, on either side, or the other. I don't know which is up or down. I find a Lidl's and get a quinoa beetroot thing and a pot of hummus, crisps, and two ciders.

Then it's time to try one of those big wafer circles that I keep seeing people eat here. They are sold everywhere in little kiosks and shops. I go to a shop that has the display in the window where they seem to be making them. I want an authentic wafer if I am going to have one.

So, I watch the lady making them for a little while. Some batter is poured into round metal plates, and then a gold-coloured, dome-shaped lid comes down. She puts the batter in the next one and the whole thing rotates. Inside the shop, there's a sweet smell. I buy a large, round wafer and walk out of the shop with it in a napkin, just the way the shopkeeper gave it to me. I take a bite, it's OK, wafery, and very sweet. I think it's 50% sugar. But it's what you do in Karlovy Vary, eat big circles and drink hot water from the ground. I have done both now. I am so glad that I brought some normal water with me to wash it down with.

On my way back to the hotel, a couple walks past me. The girl looks about 25, has a bruised eye, and clasps her boyfriend's hand tightly. I have a strange feeling. There's something unnatural about her body language, and when my eyes meet hers, I see something that I recognise. There's nothing I can do, nothing anyone can do. My abuse was private in my marriage. I struggled alone, trying to process the things that happened to me. The one time that I had anything visual to show, a huge bruise on one side of my face around my eye, I felt embarrassed. It wasn't the worst thing that had ever happened, because not all abuse is physical, but it was the first visual thing that everyone else could see. Up until that point, no one had a clue, and now it became public. But even then, nothing happened. No one insisted that I went to the police or left him. No one. Part of me wished they had. I felt shame, so much shame and I invented a story about falling over some boxes.

My friends have since said they wish that I had told them so that they could have helped. But I just didn't know how to communicate with anyone about it. It's not something to drop into a conversation. Maybe that's why I have kept friends at a distance, in case they guessed. It's so complicated.

The day after my marriage ended two friends, Cathy and Abi, came round for a Chinese which had been planned for weeks and I didn't see any need to cancel it. I think I was in shock or just numb to everything, even my marriage ending, and probably depressed.

But they came round. We ate the food, chatted, laughed, caught up, and after about an hour and a half, they asked how things were with me. I said that my marriage ended last night, and that I went to bed about 3.00 am after filling out a police report. They were shocked on so many levels, and disappointed that they hadn't been able to help me because I hadn't asked.

I just don't do drama. I hate feeling raw in front of people, hate people looking at me as if I am a project that needs fixing. I have always worked everything out in my own way.

The lady in casualty in the middle of the night asked what had happened to me and I said my husband had hit me. She said I would have to report it. I didn't know what to do. If I reported him, he would be even angrier than before and I might get hurt even worse. My kids needed me. I didn't necessarily want my marriage to end. Things were improving, except for this setback.

But I have to accept the decisions that I made back then. They felt right at the time. I just hope this girl makes the right decisions for her. Every situation is different, which is why it's so complicated.

I wander through a couple of streets that I haven't been on, that run parallel with the river but one road behind. I walk onto an ornate promenade where a couple of musicians are playing. I can almost picture how exotic this place might have been years ago. It has a lovely feel to it.

Back at the hotel, I read my Kindle on the balcony and then have a snack of hummus and beetroot on the bed. Both have a lot of chilli in, which is a shame as I can't eat too much of it. I couldn't read the ingredients, which is a bit annoying.

I open the wine, go to back to the balcony and enjoy it while watching all the tiny people on the street below, meandering up and down along the river as I did.

People look up at me, maybe not me, just up at the vista. I must look funny, sat on a chair on this tiny balcony, half in and half out of the room. I haven't seen anyone else come out on their balcony and there are other people here. I saw them at breakfast. The hotel feels extremely quiet, which is maybe why

I got such a good room, but you'd think there would be more people enjoying this view.

I do like this place. The only thing wrong, in my opinion, is the horse and carriages that go up and down all day. They should be banned. The horses are walking in the road and they look so tired and sad, carrying people who want another experience without giving a second thought to the lives these horses must live. I can hear the clip-clop of their feet all the way up here as we are in a valley.

The church next to me chimes again, it chimes often. I had a little peep earlier on the way back home and its very pretty inside.

Ciara rings me. She is having fun at Calvin's house in Bad Kreuznach, near Frankfurt.

I talk to Ciara while on the balcony. Calvin has gone to work, and she is chilling at his house. He is laughing at her German as she has an English accent and he thinks it's funny. When she leaves Calvin's place she is going to Bremen to see Cesar, her friend from Newquay, and his brother. She is exploring Bad Kreuznach and is later going to Calvin's parents in Oberwesel where they live, and where she met Calvin at the ice cream stand. He will drive her to Mainz tomorrow and then I will see her.

I watch the sunset again from my balcony and it gets chilly so I move inside. It's back to euros tomorrow and I have just got my head around the koruna. The Czech Republic is a place I feel I want to explore more. I love the countryside, the people, the quirky trains. I definitely want to come back.

I write up my Facebook post and read my Kindle until bedtime. It was a lovely, chilled day in a very unusual place.

Karlovy Vary to Mainz
Tuesday 25th August

Today is going to be a disaster, I can feel it. I got woken at 6.45 am by construction work and try very hard to let the annoyance evaporate. I am just so glad that I had my chill day yesterday. What a blessing that was, so the noise today is OK. I just wasn't expecting it. I shower and go down for breakfast.

While eating watermelon at a table for one, I check my Interrail planner. I am not getting into Mainz until 8.00 pm. How did that happen? I thought it was 6.00 pm. That means I won't see Ciara until really late tonight and she gets in during the day, and will have nothing to do but wait for me. It's bad time management on my part and I am very frustrated with myself.

I look at a map on my phone. I am going halfway across Germany. Maybe I should have stopped off somewhere else on the way. But now I have a hotel booked with Ciara and I want to spend as much time with her as I can. So, I swiftly have breakfast, butter some rolls for the train, and go back to my room with a mug of tea. No one stops me.

Upstairs, I can't find the lock for my padlock. I always keep my bag locked, even in hotel room. I search my small bag, and I can't find it. I check my wash cube, where it sometimes lives, check my shoes, another hidey place. If I can't get into my bag then I can't pack. I certainly did chill yesterday, -I didn't even pack but I thought I was getting the 12.00 pm train, that I would have all morning to get ready.

I tip the entire contents of my bag out on the floor and see my lock is tucked right in the corner. What a relief. Now, to pack and get out of here. There might be an earlier bus to Cheb. I got the bus here because of the delays on the train, but I could get a train back. I don't feel in control today.

I walk the 30 minutes to the bus and train station; but at least I know the way now. As I approach it, tI see a bus with 'Cheb' on the front, so I pop into the train station quickly to see if there is an earlier train. The lady says 12.01 pm. Hmm, I go back out to the bus, that seems the best option. The bus driver says it's going to Prague. I don't know if he stops at Cheb, or whether he hasn't changed the destination on the display. I am confused and I don't have the language to enquire more.

So, I go back to the train station and admit to myself that I have messed up. Now I have a long wait, which is sad, as I want to get going and see Ciara. I try to buy a ticket but the lady says it goes from the other train station. What other train station? Why are there two train stations?

She doesn't speak good English, and I don't have any data. She says, 'Bridge, market, 10 minutes,' and walks her fingers. I am very grateful for her English and her few important words.

I take a deep breath and go. The bridge is obvious, going over the train tracks, so you can't miss it. I go over that and then run out of clues. I am on a big road junction, and there are no footpaths. I don't know what to do. I have to make a decision, so I turn right as the road bends, not knowing what lies ahead. Maybe it's a train station. No, it's the wrong way, and I end up at a petrol station.

I retrace my steps and go left but now what? I stand on the busy roadside, sad and frustrated and tired. It's been a whirlwind this morning. My bag is heavy and I am running out of enthusiasm. If I get lost and miss my train, I might not get to Mainz at all today. I have put myself under enormous pressure.

Then, on a building up the road slightly, I see a tiny white sign with a train on it. Hooray. It should be less than 10 minutes now. With a new spring in my step, I follow the sign. But it goes into a wooded area like I am going for a bike ride and a picnic. It doesn't feel like a path to a train station. I come to a junction and have to make a decision and, of course, there are no signs to help me. A sign here would be very useful. I trust my gut instinct, which might be a mistake, but it's 50-50.

I pass a man on the footpath having a wee, how strange. I scuttle past quickly and then I see a brand new shiny train station, very different to the one over the road. It has an enormous modern bridge going over the tracks. I go up so many steps that my legs feel like jelly. There is a train on one of the platforms so I go down in a glass lift and look at the digital display. It's not my train. Now I go down under the platform, past the man who had the wee in the bush. Then back up two flights of stairs to a big digital display and some seats. There are a lot of ups and downs here.

I collapse in a chair and get my bag off my back. It's 10.16 am. There is a train earlier than I thought, which is good, but it's 15 minutes late. It would have left at 10.56 am but it will now go at 11.10 am, almost an hour away. Now that I have Wi-Fi, I re-check my trains and I still have an hour's wait on my route, so this delay is not going to affect me. At least I am at a train station and there is a train in the next hour, earlier than the 12.01 pm. Hopefully I have gained a little time, or at least not lost any. I just wish I had researched this bit better, got out of the hotel by 9.00 am and caught a 10.00 am train. Or even skipped Karlovy Vary and got into Germany. I haven't planned this bit very well. I was in such a hurry to book something and enjoy Český Krumlov that I didn't put my usual effort in, and this is the result. But I can't change that now and Karlovy Vary was a very interesting place that I would never have normally visited.

Travelling so far in one day has just put me under enormous pressure.

As soon as the platform is announced, I go down to the train. It is exactly the same train that I saw earlier. It's been there the whole time. It eventually leaves at 11.16 am and I guess it was waiting for a connecting train as my empty carriage gets invaded by four large people with rucksacks larger than mine. I put my face mask on and do my best anti-social stare. I am not in the mood today. They put their bags on the chairs and all stand in the corridor to look out of the window. If their train was delayed, they are probably just happy to have got their connection.

The second train from Cheb to Marktredwitz is a lovely new train, and I haven't seen passport control yet. We must be in Germany now, as Cheb was right on the border. The countryside is green and full of pine trees. The language on the train is definitely German. I don't know any German but I do recognise it, which is more than can be said for all the other languages from Czech Republic, Hungary, Croatia and Slovenia that all melted into one.

The connection between Pegnitz and Nuremberg is a bus, and it's very efficient, if a little scary. The driver doesn't hang about. It's all motorway, and he is overtaking container lorries. I eat my bread roll, with no banana today, and try to keep my mind off the crash that might happen.

Nuremberg station is huge. I think I have seen 22 platforms. The many digital displays that I pass in the underground corridor between the platforms remind me of my dad and all the postcards he used to send us from his work trips to this part of the world. The names all look familiar, which is strange as I have never been to this part of the world before, just Berlin once in 1990 shortly after the wall came down. Munich, Strasbourg, Stuttgart, Frankfurt. I can picture my postcards and my dad's handwriting. He never wrote much on the postcards, sometimes just one sentence: 'A plane for you,' or 'A flower for you,' but I did enjoy receiving them. And I kept them for many years.

The next train, my fourth, is to Wurzburg. It's a very posh train, the seats seem to have much more space between them and there's a handy digital display hanging from the ceiling in front of me. The Germans have nice trains. I relax and the ticket inspector arrives. I haven't seen any customs officer since getting to Germany. Oh well, the ticket man is happy.

The seats are very spacious. It's such a contrast, and they have little head pillows. I look a bit more closely and I see a Number One on the head pillow. Oops. I am in the first class carriage. No wonder it's posh, clean and so spacious. Oh well, the ticket inspector has been and seen my ticket, so I sit back and enjoy the comfort, a shame it's not a longer journey.

One more train and I arrive in Mainz, quickly heading for the entrance of the station. I get a text from Ciara asking where I am, as she is on the platform waiting for me. I race back to the platform and meet her halfway. Duh.

It is so lovely to see her happy and relaxed. She takes a photo with the Mainz sign behind us and we walk to the hotel, which she already checked into earlier this afternoon. It feels strange not looking at my phone for directions. I usually get myself to the hotel on my own, but here I am with Ciara, and she knows the way.

Time is getting on and, after dropping my bag in the hotel room, we go straight out for a stroll. Ciara takes another full-length photo of me. We look for something to eat but a lot of places are full and Ciara is a strict vegan. It's vegan or nothing. Mainz is a big place, very city-like and full of large buildings. We take a quick walk down to the Rhine, which puts a smile on my face. I have always wanted to visit it, maybe cruise along, and now I am standing on the edge. Mainz is an interesting place.

We end up in a burrito place which is a gamble, as neither of us does spicy food but Ciara came here with Calvin, so she knows it's going to be OK. I am surprised how much I enjoy it.

Ciara is lovely company. I haven't had any company or conversation for weeks except ordering food and train tickets and asking for kettles. I don't know any German, except, '*Eine tasse kaffee, bitte,*' which a work friend, Tina, taught me and I don't even drink coffee. I can't even read a menu, so I need Ciara's help. She has passed her GCSE and is very keen to learn German, which is partly why she's here now. She tries to order the food and does well, but the staff are busy and sometimes reply in English to speed the process up. But she tries and I can see her confidence building.

When we get back to the hotel, she asks the receptionist in German for a kettle. She had googled the word for kettle. The lady gives us a kettle but not a cup, so I ask Ciara to ask for a cup and say '*tasse,*' and we both laugh. The four words that I learnt when I was 21 have come in handy at last.

I go to sleep in Germany, having woken up in the Czech Republic.

Mainz

Wednesday 26th August

There's no breakfast to get up to at this hotel, so me and Ciara chill in our room. I drink a few cups of green tea and have some biscuits. Luckily, Ciara has her own snacks as mine have milk in them. I just haven't bothered trying to read the ingredients in all the different countries.

Ciara, who is a whizz on the internet, as are all kids her age, looks at flights home for me. She is much faster and more efficient than me. I use the time to book a night in Koblenz. It's the next major town on the map and seems the best choice. I am not that excited about it, which is why I have only booked one night, but at least I know where I am going next.

I am a bit sad as I don't want to get a flight home. I think I have more chance of picking up the virus on a plane than a train and I really enjoyed my train journey on the Eurostar. I wanted to do the whole trip on land. Plus, this is more money. But this is a pandemic and I chose to travel in it, so it is what it is. And I am counting my blessings that, so far on this trip I haven't had any disasters, so if this is the only thing that hasn't gone to plan, then it's OK. I have had such a fantastic time, that I am not in a position to moan. The flights look very expensive when I researched yesterday, but Ciara manages to get me one for £119 from Cologne. So, Cologne is now my last destination.

We leave the room at about 12.00 pm and go straight to the vegan place around the corner which I am very happy about.

I prefer to eat vegan for all the usual reasons, better for me, having read *The China Study* and seen the documentary *Forks over Knives*. Also, better for the environment and better for the animals. Liam, Aidan, and Ciara got around Europe eating 100% vegan, but I have different priorities. Plus, they cooked and ate a lot of pasta in the hostels and went to bigger cities than me where it is easier to find vegan food. I have eaten meat for 50 years. So, the fact I don't now, except for rare occasions, has to be a huge improvement. This might be my only trip to Europe and I want to eat what I want to eat and not feel bad about it. The best food that I have had on this trip has been in vegan places like the one in Ljubljana and the one in Bled, which was in another league.

Mohren Milieu is not far from our hotel. We sit outside at the wooden tables, feeling a slight chill. It's difficult to comprehend that, not that long ago, I was melting in the heat in Venice. I have travelled a long way, and the weather has changed as I moved around Europe.

I have a burger with wedges and it's yummy, and Ciara has a buddha bowl. I would have loved a piece of vegan cake but I am full. This is our breakfast really, not lunch.

Then we go off to explore. So far, Mainz hasn't been what I pictured. It's not that pretty, and it has a city feel. I saw a photo of an old part of town when I was researching where to stay and I want to find that bit. We find the right area and take some photos. It's small and the photo I take is the same as what I saw on the internet, so it's not like there are streets and streets of photo opportunities. But it's pretty and old, with half-timbered, attractive buildings and cobble stone streets.

We find some shops and Ciara buys a children's book in German. I buy a new top in the charity shop as my clothes all smell like they have been washed in the sink for weeks, which they have. And I buy a new journal as I have filled the other three up.

We find a church with a huge door called St Augustine's Church. I stand in front of it to have my photo taken and Ciara has to move a long way back to get the door in, I look tiny, tinier than normal.

The inside is beautiful. The artwork on the ceiling is breath-taking with soft floaty, delicate colours. The walls are painted white with ornate paintings, in delicate blues and pinks and framed with gold, covering the entire ceiling. There are many large windows letting in lots of light to illuminate the church. I can't believe you can just walk in off the street and see such amazing paintings. If I lived here, I would come in every day. This is a treat. The inside isn't huge and it is just off the street, so we could easily have missed it. It's a bit of a surprise and I am really glad that we came in.

After this, we walk along by the Rhine. Calvin had told Ciara that there's a little beach over the other side and I quite fancy crossing the Rhine. It's not every day you can do that. I stop halfway across and with the wind blowing my hair about, I manage to collect the three little words. We find the little empty beach. It isn't lifeguard attended but there is a stack of deck chairs, so we help ourselves and sit down to chill. It is lovely to relax with Ciara and I have someone to talk to, which makes me realise how little I have been talking these last three weeks.

Ciara reads me her new little children's book and it takes her a while. She has to google the words that she doesn't know and then she pieces the sentences together. She reads them to me one chapter at a time. It is a cute little book about painting a bedroom unit in different colours. And it's so surreal anyway, sitting on a remote tiny beach, next to the Rhine, in Germany with Ciara, that it sort of fits in.

I just sit and chill. There are swans sitting down on the edge of the water, chilling as well.

We walk back over the bridge and into a strange outdoor café to use the loo, but it all seems too weird to stop and get a drink. It's probably perfect on a sunny day when it's buzzing with people. But we have to fill in COVID-19 forms just to get in, even though we aren't actually 'in' anywhere, we are outdoors. It doesn't feel very welcoming, so we use the loo and quickly escape.

We have a bit of trouble finding somewhere to eat our evening meal. Some places are full, or the menu isn't as it said on the internet, but we do find a nice upstairs place that looks good. As soon as we sit down, I need the loo, so walk back towards the entrance where the toilets are. When I get there, I have to choose between two doors with the letters 'D' or 'G'. I have no idea and making the wrong choice would be bad, so I go back to our table at the far end and ask Ciara which door to go in. I would have chosen the wrong door, so I am glad that I asked her.

It's so lovely to have dinner with someone, especially my own daughter, and have a catch-up. She is so keen to learn German that she is seriously thinking about moving here. She googles job opportunities while we wait for our dinner, and reads them out to me. She says she feels really at home here. I am not getting it, but we are completely different people. She does well ordering our food in German and I can see her confidence growing, she is very determined.

Ciara is a qualified mental health nurse and I don't balk at her saying she wants to pack it in and become an *au pair* or work on a farm. This is because, at 21 years old, she got cancer, which is always life changing, but to have it so young must be difficult to process and completely change your outlook on life. As her mother, I have struggled to process it, and support her through a really nasty operation. I feel in my heart that it's her life and she should choose what she wants to do with it. I am happy that she has the confidence and the ability to question what she wants. I am super proud of her.

The pizza is good, absolutely full of toppings – the small cherry tomatoes roll off. It's delicious, as is the glass of pink wine that I have with it.

We walk back to the hotel in the dark. This is the first time that I have been out in the dark on my trip and it feels a bit strange, like our roles have reversed and Ciara is looking after me.

I put some photos on Facebook and go to sleep.

Mainz to Koblenz
Thursday 27th August

We snack on biscuits for breakfast and make tea with our kettle. Ciara has an important phone call to make, which takes a while, then we pop back to the vegan place for a cuppa and a piece of cake. The trip to Mainz has been brief, but it was quality time spent with Ciara, and it flew past. She has to continue her holiday in Bad Kreuznach with Calvin, and I am moving on to Koblenz to explore some more.

We walk to the train station and it's time to say goodbye. At 1.25 pm, I am hopefully on the right train to Koblenz.

I desperately hope that this is the scenic route. I came to Mainz to see some of the scenery on the Rhine. From here to Koblenz, it should be pretty. I asked the lady at the desk for a ticket for the scenic route to Koblenz via Bingen. It's going to be nicer than getting the high-speed train to Koblenz. I am not in any hurry and I want to see some views.

The journey is half an hour long before I stop at Bingen, and then another half hour more. I am a bit excited to have a train journey along the Rhine. I get comfortable in my seat and get my camera ready but there's a strange atmosphere on the train. Everyone is on their phones, and no one is looking out of the window.

At 1.46 pm, all I can see are houses. It's quite possible that I am on the wrong train, despite telling the ticket lady that I wanted the scenic route. Drat.

I am learning German though, the train stops every few minutes and says, 'Nachster Halt,' which must mean, 'Next Stop.'

I can see lovely sloping hills in the distance, but there are lots of buildings in the way. I can't imagine there is another train track that runs the same way. Maybe there is. The next section is pretty, but I am not blown away. I sit back, a little disappointed.

But then the next section is better, not like the Panoramic-Express in Switzerland because that had a different colour palette to anywhere that I have ever been before. But this is pretty. The train runs along the Rhine which is what I wanted. I am sitting on the edge of my seat taking photos while everyone else is going to work or going home. This is not the first time this has happened on this trip.

I get off at Bingen. I was hoping to get a cup of tea or a drink, but I seem to have missed the stop I wanted. Typical. There was a bridge in the photo I looked at before that had some buildings in it and I was hoping to stop there. But there's nothing here except the station and lots of flat landscapes, fields and then the Rhine. Oh well, I have half an hour or as long as I want, so I go for a stroll. I have to go down the bridge steps and onto ground level, across a field. There is a small takeaway, but it's not what I pictured and only two people are sitting there.

I walk to the edge of the Rhine where it's very peaceful, as no one is here. The gently sloping hills on the edge of the river are quite stunning. This isn't where I wanted to be, having got off at the wrong stop, but this is incredibly special. It's so silent, the gentle hills frame the Rhine and there are white fluffy clouds in the blue sky. I am very lucky to be here.

When I am done, I walk back and get the next train. My bag is heavy and I am happy to move on. I did consider going back one stop and getting off where I planned to go, but I am going to move forward.

We arrive in Koblenz. Thank goodness I have data as I go the wrong way when I leave the train station, before correcting myself. It's very built-up and feels like a city, but I think it's just a big town. The hotel is not that far from the train station. I picked a good location again.

The hotel is OK, nothing special, but I am thinking of stopping one more night. I am only booked in for one, but it's €70 a night, which is a lot for what you get, and more than I want to spend. The lady at reception is a little gruff. When I go back down and ask about a kettle, as there isn't one in my room, she says that I can't have one because of COVID-19. But her attitude feels like she is accusing me of not realising that there's a pandemic on and she simply can't let me have a kettle in my room.

I am tempted to let her know where in Europe I have had a kettle in my room, but think twice about it. I have to respect the fact that every business is dealing with this strange situation the best that they can. She offers to boil the kettle for me whenever I want, so I can't complain, except I have to wander up and down the stairs again with my hot water. That seems a little daft to me but that's their rules. I drink a lot of tea and I am probably going to annoy her.

I have googled where to eat as I am really hungry. Google Maps takes me to a vegan café about 15 minutes away. It's a really hot day and I sit out the front with my sunglasses on, next to the main road. I have a fizzy blackcurrant which is good. I have that a lot at home. This one has a sprig of rosemary in it, which is a little unnecessary, but it looks nice. It's a busy road, so there's nothing much to look at, but I am here for the food. I have a hearty salad, sat in the sunshine. It's packed with nutrients and I feel a lot better for it.

I then set off in search of the Rhine again and end up in a residential area on a peninsula, but it's the wrong peninsula and you can only get across by ferry. So, I backtrack and eventually get to where I thought I was heading the first time and walk on a lovely promenade along the river.

A row of tall trees lines the path with more rows of posh houses to my left, the Rhine to my right. It's very peaceful and families are lying on the grass, kids are playing, some people are drinking alcohol. It's all very nice and civilised. It's a lovely walk. I like it here.

The Rhine is pretty. I can see the houses on the other side, and the water is very blue and calm. Then a castle comes into view at the top of the hill on the opposite side of the river and I see a cable car going up to it, over the river. I want to go up in that cable car. It looks lots of fun. It's getting a bit late now to do that, so on the spot, I decide I will have to stop another night.

I walk to the very end at a point where the Rhine meets the Moselle at this triangular point, with water on all sides. I arrive at a huge statue, the biggest that I have ever seen. It's of a man on a horse, already large enough but they have perched it on top of a huge monument. It's massive.

Everyone is taking photos. There's a lot to see from all sides, and this is a significant point on a map. It is such a lovely spot. The sun is shining and I feel privileged to be here. I decide to try and get up on the monument as I can see other people up there too. You can get to the stone that the horse is perched on. There are many steps, but when you climb up, you can see the triangle, and I get some great photos of where the two rivers meet. I take a couple of bad selfies, squinting in the sunshine. I walk back down from the statue, turn left and walk on the Moselle side, and find my way into the town and the shops.

Koblenz seems to have everything: nature, cable cars, rivers, statues and a great shopping centre, plus an old bit of town and lots of history. It's all very clean and civilised. I think Ciara would like it here, I think it's more interesting than Mainz.

I pop into what looks like a mini-market, but it has foods that I don't know. In fact, most of it I don't recognise, it's a nationality that I am not familiar with but they have some lovely looking plums, so I get a bagful and some unusual looking crisps, and a Diet Coke. It's the only drink I see in the fridge that I recognise. I don't drink Coke much and it's the first on this trip so it will make a change from Fanta and fizzy water.

Using my data and Google Maps, I find my way back to the hotel and get back at about 7.00 pm. I book an extra night, although it's such a shame it's so expensive. I think it's just city prices because it's nothing special.

I wait downstairs for the man to boil the kettle and then get the lift back up two flights in case I spill the water. I have a shower, wash some clothes and hang them in the shower, hoping that they will dry. I wash all my plums and leave them to dry on a clean towel.

The glass of Coke is very tasty and goes well with the very weird sweetcorn-flavoured crisps. They are strange, but edible, and I am not sure if I like them but I carry on eating.

Now that I have a flight, I can book the rest of my trip and fill in the gap, so I do some research. I am almost at Cologne now, probably an hour or two on the train, so I am restricted as to where I can go unless I get a train a bit further away and come back into Cologne. But I won't have any Interrail days left to do that. Also, I don't want to spend four nights in a big city.

I google pretty places to stay on the Rhine, and there is quite a list. It makes perfect sense to spend some more time in this area, in a small town rather than a big city. I am spoilt for choice, most of them would be lovely, but I decide to stop in Bacharach. I like the name and it looks lovely and it has good reviews on the internet. I look for a hotel, and one or two look suitable but the reviews aren't that good. I keep coming back to one in particular and it has a single room, which might be small, but the hotel looks really special. It is a similar price to this one and has bags of character. This has zero.

So, I will be going back half an hour south on the train. It looks a cute little place. I am excited again now. I want to enjoy the last few days and this seems a great idea.

I post on Facebook and I speak to Phil for almost an hour and we have a lovely natter. Then I go to sleep, I have a cable car to get in the morning.

Koblenz
Friday 28th August

I wake up to the noises of a busy street; trains, people, and traffic, but I did sleep well. I go down for breakfast, not knowing what to expect. Yesterday I had to book a time slot as they are trying to do it in shifts to avoid overcrowding. Breakfast costs an extra €6.00 but I felt badgered into it. The hotel is already expensive enough without paying more for breakfast. My gut feeling was right, it isn't good. I said that I didn't eat meat, and they have laid out a pile of meat, a boiled egg, bread, and jam on my table.

The tea is good and the juice is tasty. I have two brown rolls with jam on. I leave the egg and meat untouched. It will probably go in the bin, which annoys me. But it is what it is, I won't have breakfast tomorrow.

I go back to my room, pack my bag for my morning out, and go in search of a cable car. The bread is sitting heavy in my tummy. I am not eating bread for ages when I get home.

To avoid any rushes, and because I am excited to get a cable car over the Rhine up to a castle, I go straight there and get a ticket. The cable cars are big, with a huge concrete station they pivot round, collect their passengers and go back to the castle. It's still early and very quiet and I get on a cable car without any queuing. I share it with a couple a little older than me. I take photos and enjoy the ride up to the top, looking at the great views down onto the river and of the huge statue.

I get off and walk across a lawn to the castle, which I learn is actually a fortress. There is very little staff about. I don't get offered a map or any information, and most of the plaques are in German. I wander around, not knowing what I am looking at. The walls are incredibly tall. It's an enormous old fortress with deep walls. I wander around aimlessly, but it doesn't really light my fire. I am probably missing most of it, but I am impressed by its sheer size and importance. There's no escaping that.

The view from the platform up high is great. I am more into views than history and this view is stunning. The statue of the man on a horse looks tiny from up here. I must find out who he is. After about an hour I am done, it's not my kind of history and without any help to understand it, I give up and get the cable car back down.

There's hardly any staff here as it's an automated gate, and it's going so slow that you just walk on, no staff required. I time it so that I jump on and I get the whole car to myself. I am thrilled. I look around this big glass bubble and giggle to myself. I take even more photos going down than I took going up. I put my bag down on the bench, walk around the cable car, look out all the windows, take selfies and just laugh. It's so much fun on my own, hovering over the Rhine in this glass bubble. This has been such an amazing trip, you just never know what's going to happen next.

It's over way too quickly. I would like to go back up and down again. But, too soon, my huge glass bubble car docks and I have to get off. I am still smiling as I walk away from it.

I decide to go back to my hotel for a much-needed cup of tea. The man at the desk is very nice and chats while the kettle is boiling. He gives me my water in a cup on a tray and I get the lift up again. I go back to my room, look at my photos, drink my tea, and fall asleep. I get woken up by a Facebook notification, which is probably a blessing.

The weather looks like it's turning, and it looks particularly bad on Sunday. I need to buy a new coat as I left mine in Morzine. I have noticed the weather getting cooler as I have moved up through Germany.

I hate shopping, but I do need a coat. I go into the huge shopping mall with an interesting exterior. It appears to be covered in pretend grass, so it looks very green. And I spot noodles on the top floor amongst the food offerings. I love noodles and have enjoyed the ones in the shopping mall at Budejovice. Even when they were cold, they were delicious. The vegetarian ones are €3.00, too good to miss. I sit in the big eating area full of chairs and tables, socially distanced after filling in my name on a piece of paper.

The noodles are not amazing, unfortunately but they are hot and cheap. I eat all the veg and leave quite a lot of noodles as they are a bit thick and heavy, very different from the thin yummy ones in Budejovice.

After that, I find a coat in the second clothes shop that I go in, which is a result. It is €10, so I can't go wrong. It's not a coat that I would buy normally, it's bordering on hideous and is very badly made, as you would expect for €10. But it's a lightweight coat that looks warm and, more importantly, squashes up very small.

Then I go for a walk down the Moselle side. It's not as pretty as the Rhine, at least not this section. I expect it is further down. There are lots of those narrow, two-storey river cruise boats parked. I have always wanted to go on one of these, so I have a good look at all the different styles and take a few photos to record the brands. I think a cruise up the Rhine on one of these long boats would be fun.

I decide to stop for a drink by the river but the first place is full of beer drinkers, and the second is in the shade. I feel a bit fussy, but it's not just about the drink. I need to feel comfortable when I sit down somewhere. So, I walk past the big statue. I see a kiosk with chairs outside and the menu says they have tea and I ask the lady what sort of milk she has. She sort of sighs, rummages under the counter, and produces a little UHT pot. No, I can't, that's not going to work for me. I walk away, feeling like Goldilocks. It would be so much easier if I drank coffee. I am definitely in the minority.

Then I see a little row of hotels with chairs and tables out the front. They are facing the river and the fortress. One of the hotels has a beautiful display of flowers, three rows of deep fuchsia flowers at the front of the building. It has no customers, whereas the other hotels do. I know what it's like to have a business and no customers, so I decide to stop there and have a drink.

I order an apple spritzer, which turns out to be an apple juice with no spritz. I chill, watching the people going by and it's good to sit down, I have done a fair bit of walking today. It's almost 5.00 pm and I am not sure what to do now.

My flight home is on Wednesday morning. I have tonight here, and two nights in Bacharach on Saturday and Sunday, so I need to think about Monday and Tuesday. The flight is very early, and I was going to stay at the airport all night, so I only need one night's accommodation.

Maybe I could even book a hostel in Cologne. I need to do some research and see where I get the train to the airport from, and if they do a late-night train. I don't especially want to travel late at night, but I probably don't have a lot of choice.

But if I only get one night at a hostel, I will be carrying my rucksack around from noon, when I leave the hostel all through the day and into the night. So maybe I should get two nights: at least then I don't have to carry it about all day. There's not much point economising now. I have spent a fortune on the trip, and

I will hate my bag if I have to carry it all day and I am quite fond of it at the moment.

I also need to think about where I am staying in Cornwall and sort a COVID-19 test out, so I can hopefully get a negative test and go home to Phil. It's not quite the ending I pictured.

Right, that's enough here, I am going for a wander again. The sun is trying to peep out and I need to make the most of my time here in Koblenz.

I look for somewhere to eat in a social, bustling part of town which has a lot of eating places and I fail. I find sitting down at a restaurant or café really difficult. It has to feel right. The menu has to be good, with sensible prices and good food choices. The chairs have to be comfy, the light has to be right. It's surprising that I have ever sat down anywhere to eat. I am hungry and want something hot, but I just can't make a decision.

I felt very comfortable at the last place by the river, but I get bored as well when I am on my own, because obviously there is no scintillating conversation. The surroundings are not so important when you are with someone that you want to be with. But on your own, it has to be right. So, after looking at a few menus, checking out the atmosphere, the chairs and the lighting, I am back at the hotel making a banana roll from the one I took from breakfast with the portion size margarine from another hotel, possibly Český Krumlov, and the banana that I bought yesterday in the supermarket. It's not very ripe and I am cross with myself for not having sat down at one of those places for a warm bowl of chips.

I haven't eaten well today, and it's my own fault. I have a cup of tea to go with my chewy banana roll and then take a shower. I think have done Koblenz; my tracker says that I walked over 11 miles today.

I am looking forward to Bacharach. I had an email to say there will be a kettle in my room. Result. If you don't ask, you don't get.

Koblenz to Bacharach
Saturday 29th August

I liked Koblenz, but this hotel is bland and one that will slip from my memory the fastest. It's a great location and perfectly OK, but I have been to far better on this trip. Karlovy Vary and Český Krumlov will be etched in my memory forever. I really would like a cup of tea, but they will be busy with breakfast downstairs, so it's best not to bother them for hot water.

I can't get into the new hotel until 3.00 pm and it's only half an hour's journey on the train back along the Rhine. The instructions in my room say that I need to be out of here by 10.45 am which is very specific. They will probably charge you another whole day if you go down at 11.00 am.

There's no Welcome Pack here, just four pages of rules and what not to do, which is very harsh and probably very German. Ciara said she likes the Germans because they say it how it is and she feels comfortable with that. I don't feel the same. I have broken one of the rules by hanging my knickers up to dry.

I couldn't get to sleep until about 2.00 am as the noisy couple next door came crashing in at 12.30 am and I thought I was going to hear the bed moving, but they decided to talk all night. The lift is also very noisy and just outside the door. It's a really old lift that creaks and it felt like everyone used it last night. I eat my delicious plums for my breakfast, but I want a cup of tea.

At 10.30 am, I go and hand in my keys and make my way to the train station.

I arrive in Bacharach at 12.15 pm after a nice short train ride. When I get off, I feel like I have walked into a beautiful painting. The street you find yourself on after coming out of the train station is narrow, and the buildings all look medieval with their top halves timbered with dark wood against the cream walls. It reminds me of Fowey and I'm not sure why, it's nothing like it, but the houses on both sides are quite close together with a narrow road. And it runs parallel with the river, like Fowey, but you can't see it. It's full of character.

I find my hotel, and it's the most stunning building here in Bacharach. It's called Altkolnischer Hof and I can't wait to get in, but it's far too early.

I wander about and it doesn't take me long to realise that it's a very small place and I have walked around it already. That's quite comforting because Koblenz was a big place with a lot of exploring and walking. This is just one street, full of pretty timber-framed houses and hotels and, of course, the river on the other side of the road.

My backpack is hurting, so I find a little café on the main street. It's got a lovely atmosphere and I feel right at home here. It feels like it's someone's front room and it's very quirky. The walls are full of photos and the low window ledge is full: copper items and wooden barrels, antique-styled things, and shelves full of teapots and bits and bobs. I wouldn't want to dust in here.

The owner is lovely. I order a green tea and a piece of apple cake. It's perfect. I feel like I am having a cuppa in their front room, surrounded by all their knick-knacks. I must learn a little German, or at least enough to read a menu. I can't understand a thing. I can manage in Spain and France with a menu, but not here. German feels like a language that I should know a little bit more of.

Just as I am thinking about paying as I have been here a while now, four of the staff sit down at a table at the far end and eat their dinner. It looks like the lady who served me is the owner, with her husband, and maybe the other two are staff, or possibly a son and daughter. So, I sit back and chill. They don't seem very put out that I am still here.

I eventually pay and go down to the water, passing under a bridge and crossing a road until I am on the waterside. A footpath that runs along the Rhine and I find a bench, slip my backpack off and take it all in. Here I am back at the Rhine. I sit and watch the boats going up and down. It's very peaceful and not at all built-up. This was a very good decision.

I decide to go to my hotel and ask if I can leave my bag there so that I can walk around until it's time to book in. By some miracle, they let me into my room two hours early. I am so glad that I asked.

The room is perfect and couldn't be a bigger contrast to the bland room of yesterday. This is modern, posh, and historic all rolled into one. This room has a kettle on a little tray, it has a fridge, an internet tablet with details of the hotel and how to book a table at dinner or talk to reception. It's beautifully decorated with a big stunning photo of the Rhine, in a frame that has a light over my bed. I have a reading lamp, and the bathroom is top of the range, with a colourful autumnal photo of the Rhine on the backdrop of the shower. I have never seen anything like it.

It's only a single room, but it's an amazing single room, very comfortable and snug, and not that small. I am chuffed to pieces. My luck just keeps giving. I think Uncle Bob is up there sorting out my holiday for me. It certainly feels incredible to have had so much luck on this trip: the weather, the choice of accommodation and the amazing experiences.

Unfortunately, I can't get the kettle to work, but I only just had one at the café, so I pick up my bag and go to explore. I mention to the lad at the reception that the kettle won't work, and he asks if I have put the key card in the slot to activate the electricity. Duh, I have been in a variety of hotels recently, and all of them have had a key to the door, so I didn't think. That's good. The kettle works and I look a bit silly, I can cope with that.

I have already walked the length of the village and been to the river, so this time I turn right out of the hotel and walk up a residential street, still pretty but with fewer historic buildings. I find myself climbing a bit of a hill. I am not sure where I am going, just exploring. Soon, I have to make a decision at a junction in the road and I turn left. This takes me on a hairpin bend with no footpath and up a hill. It gets quite steep, and I am not sure whether to carry on or not as I don't know where I am going. I turn on my data and look at Google Maps and it looks like it turns right at the end. I have turned and I am now facing the water, although I can't see it. I decide to go to the edge and see if there is a nice view, as I have come this far.

I find a little viewing platform and take some photos. I send a photo to Ciara. She says she has gone out for the day with one of Calvin's friends. She was going to be part of a camping trip this weekend but her lack of German sort of got in the way. So, she is staying at his friend's house, which is even more bizarre than her staying with Calvin, and the friend has kindly taken her to a castle on the Rhine. It feels so strange that Ciara is having a holiday too and doing similar things. She sends me a photo back, and it's almost the same. Same height, same sort of view. Very strange. I look around me in case she is in a bush, hiding, which wouldn't surprise me.

To my left is a castle, or a hotel, I am not sure. I walk down and explore, following the footpath and a sign to the castle. You might have to pay to get in, and I am not that interested in going inside. But I walk down a narrow stone path in the castle grounds and end up at an outdoor seating area with the most phenomenal view of the Rhine. And in the middle is a kiosk selling snacks and drinks. Life couldn't get any better right now.

I plonk my bag onto a table and go and get a drink. I was going to have tea but in a spontaneous moment I order a glass of local Riesling. It seems the most appropriate thing to do and I return to my seat with a glass of wine.

The wine, the location, the weather, it's all perfect.

This is one of those moments in time. I used to drink a lot of German wine, but it used to make me drunk very quickly and give me a headache, so I stopped.

The flavour and the taste of the Riesling is incredible, one of my favourites, and I am at the Rhine drinking it. It's like golden nectar, and I sip every mouthful mindfully. I savour every drop on my tongue. It's crisp and cold and I look at the incredible view in front of me and breathe out.

Because I am so high up, I can see the Rhine stretch away into the distance, the gently sloping hills on either side of the bank, and Bacharach below me.

I used to have a plaque that I bought on a holiday to America that said, 'We don't remember days, we remember moments.'

This is one of those moments. I am and have been so incredibly lucky. I have enjoyed this trip so much and this feels like a highlight, but that's because it's now, I am enjoying now. I have nothing to do after this drink, nothing to do tomorrow. Time is irrelevant and now, I am here drinking this delicious German wine, looking at a fantastic view. The sun pops out of the clouds every so often to warm my face, and the wine is cool and refreshing.

I am content, and suddenly, from nowhere, tears fall silently down my face. They take me by surprise and I cannot put into words how I feel.

I feel some kind of acceptance.

I have been through what I have been through. I survived it. And life is good. I am lucky.

I know myself better. I know that I prefer nature to big cities. I had the courage to believe in what I wanted and changed my plans from Budapest and Prague to Český Krumlov, Karlovy Vary and now Bacharach, and I have been rewarded tenfold for it. This trip had to suit my personality and I think it's fitted very well.

I hope all these new memories squeeze out the box set of horrors and demote it to the back of a dusty drawer in my head. They are part of me, but hopefully, from now on they won't have a hold on me.

I wipe away the tears on my cheek, feeling a little embarrassed, but I don't think anyone has noticed. I wasn't sobbing, just a little bit of emotion leaked out.

I am not a tearful person. I learned very young when I lay in bed and my parents were arguing that nobody was coming to pacify me. The tears don't achieve anything and it just gives you a headache. I have cried silent tears when I have been caught out, but it's quite rare. One of my dad's favourite sayings after upsetting us was, 'If you don't stop crying, I'll give you something to cry about.' I never could understand the logic.

Even when Ciara told me over the phone that she had cancer, I didn't cry. She didn't cry. We were both practical; what happens next, where do we go from here. But no tears. I had some tears on my own, but not many. And it's not because I wasn't upset, clearly I was. My 21-year-old daughter had been diagnosed with cancer.

I think it's positive that I have have to wipe some tears away. Maybe, I am thawing. Maybe it's time for the numbness to go. Maybe, from now on, I will wear my heart on my sleeve, be emotional. Let it all out.

I have been emotionally numb most of my life. It's a defence mechanism. The only way I could cope with a difficult childhood and a difficult marriage was to build a huge wall around me. But I didn't want a big wall around me. I didn't even understand that it was there. But I have gone through most of my life on my own, even when I was with other people. I am comfortable being me. Other people don't always treat me right, so I keep people at arm's length. And even if I do let the wall down, the minute I feel undefended, it comes back up very fast and I retreat.

Maybe, from now on, after this amazing trip, with a new freedom from being the age I am, my children all independent, me being content and secure with Phil, maybe now I can let the wall down.

This has been more than an amazing holiday. I always wondered if it would change me. Phil asked the same and said that he hoped it wouldn't change me too much, which is one of the nicest things anyone has ever said to me. No one has really ever understood me as Phil does. Our personalities are very similar, so we find it easy to understand each other.

I feel a bit more solid as a person. I don't feel so fragile and wobbly. I still am, as you can see from the episode in Český Krumlov with the drunk men, but I have to accept that is part of me and it's not that much of a hindrance. We all have a past. It's what has made us who we are, and often bits of our past creep into our now. But that's OK.

I like me. I have a lot of good qualities. I am happy, despite my few tears. In fact, I am happier for the tears and that, in itself, is a blessing. I feel very positive about the future.

I genuinely feel like I am healing. I am excited at how life will look when I return to it. Can I keep this contentment? Have I turned a ginormous corner?

It seems ironic that I am drinking alcohol and feeling happy. Alcohol tainted my childhood and my marriage. That's a lot of years, most of my life. But I am not an alcoholic, despite me wondering about my relationship with alcohol every time I take a sip.

I finish the last delicious mouthful of wine. I would love another, but I don't think it will taste the same even if it came from the same bottle, as that was a moment in time, and it's passed.

I walk down a different way, not on the long hairpin bend that I came up from. I see a path and a signpost down to the village. I pass a couple struggling to get up the steps. This is a very difficult climb to the top. Mine was, by comparison, a gentle incline. I pass the memorial church, which has a very sad story. I stand for a few minutes, taking it all in.

I pop into the little supermarket for fizzy water. My data doesn't work and I can't figure it out, so I bravely ask a customer and he happily tells me which is best. It starts to rain on the 20 feet back to the hotel. I just can't believe again how lucky I have been with the weather.

I book a table in the restaurant for 5.30 pm on the computer in my room. What a great idea. I am starving. I ate very little yesterday and only cake so far today.

I go down and the lady on duty seats me by the window overlooking the street. There are pink cerise flowers on the window ledges. The table is set out with top-class china. It feels very luxurious, and the room is stunning, with dark wood everywhere and lovely linen on the tables. Everything is quality: the table decorations, the art on the wall. This feels like a five-star hotel and restaurant.

Stevie Wonder and The Script play over the speakers, my kind of music. Before I know it, I have ordered pork tenderloin, with chips and roast veg and mushrooms. I can only blame my hunger, the setting and the smells from the kitchen. I simply have no excuse, except, pork is my favourite meat. I haven't had it in years and if I am going to eat it, this is the place to do so, on a day where I have cried with happiness over a view. I order another glass of Riesling, wait for my food, and feel tearful again. What is wrong with me today?

I simply feel content. Even ordering the pork is a strong thing to do, obviously wrong if you preach veganism. I will never go back to eating meat every day, every week, every month, or even every year. But right now, today in this magnificent restaurant, in this beautiful hotel, it's what I want to do.

I could have pretended that I hadn't ordered pork, but I am fed up with lying. My marriage was built on lies and deceit, pretending everything was OK when it definitely wasn't. I have turned a corner; I am going to be truthful. I was in an abusive marriage, yes, I did get hurt but I am OK now. And today I had pork for my dinner. I am not lying anymore.

I eat my meal which is cooked to perfection, as I had already guessed it would be. There are swirls of red and green on my plate, pesto and homemade tomato sauce, the whole meal is outstanding. I sip the wine with my meal and I am in the restaurant for an hour and a half.

I decide against a walk, despite the rain having stopped, and go to my room. The shower is the poshest I have ever used. The photo of the Rhine really is a lovely touch. There are two shower heads again but two separate buttons and much easier to work out. The water is at a perfect temperature without me having to alter it.

I write a post on Facebook, and chill with my bed lamp on and don't even need to get up to turn the light out.

Today was amazing.

Bacharach
Sunday 30th August

Breakfast is so beautifully laid out in this handsome room that I take a photo. The table is set with beautiful plates, just like last night, with the hotel logo on them and a cute napkin. The buffet is stunning: fresh fruit, juices, jams in posh containers, and lovely bread. There is a lot to choose from and everything is of exceptional quality. I enjoy every mouthful.

There isn't much to do in Bacharach. It's tiny. Knowing this, I decide to go for a stroll along the Rhine. I walk to the river and go right and passing through a campsite full of motorhomes, and then along the footpath. To my left is a stone jetty going out across the water, so I walk along it and sit down. I think it's shallower here, and it might be to stop the boats drifting over, but I am only guessing. I am quite a way out over the river and take some photos of a cruise coming by. It's very peaceful.

I get back on the path and see lots of small plots of land. At first, I think they must be allotments, some have vegetables or fruit growing, but now they look more like back gardens that are not attached to a house. They all seem to have some kind of structure, a large garden-shed-type building and barbeque, and kids' toys. Not one person is using them as I walk by, but they all look loved and used. Maybe families come for holidays or weekends.

The vista doesn't change much. This part of the Rhine seems to look the same, whichever bit of it you are on. I try to walk to a bend up ahead, but it seems to stay the same distance away and I can't quite see around the corner, so I turn away and walk back slowly to the hotel. It is a lovely, relaxing walk.

When I get back, I realise I have locked myself out as I left the key in the electric thing. So, I have to ask the lad at reception for another key. I make a cup of tea and chill. I can feel the holiday coming to an end and I am starting to worry about the details: the COVID-19 test, cheap hotels in Cologne, and how to get to the airport for such a stupid flight time, or whether to wait in the airport overnight; either is not good. It's all getting very real now.

I am tempted to just lie on my bed all afternoon, but I force myself to go back out and turn left this time.

The sun comes out, meaning I slip off my cardigan and don't walk as far as this morning. I go just as far as I want, and then back again. It's incredibly peaceful along the Rhine, very tranquil, and this is a good time to enjoy it before my arrival in Cologne. I take a seat at a small drinking place by the river. It's also the ticket office to get a boat up the Rhine.

There aren't many places to sit by the river, so I am pleased to get a seat to watch the activities on the water. I get an apple juice and watch the boats coming and going, people getting on what look like water taxis. The bigger cruise ones just sail past. Although I have seen more cargo vessels than people ones.

By now, breakfast was a long time ago, so I decide to eat again at the hotel. I sit down at 6.30 pm, and the food can't improve on yesterday so I order the same, but I don't hang around quite as long today. I decide to go for one last stroll down by the river before I stay in for the night. I turn right as I come out of the hotel instead of left as I usually do. I haven't explored much behind the hotel. The narrow street is full of charm, more pretty houses and a bar and a restaurant.

As I walk back in front of my hotel, there is a black Porsche parked opposite the entrance. I wouldn't have known it was a Porsche except for it saying 'Porsche' right across the back of it. I am no good with cars.

I take a photo. Calvin picked Ciara up in his black Porsche from the airport. They must be popular here. I send her a message and the photo, saying, 'Have you come to visit me ... lol'. I walk down to the water and sit for a while, enjoying the stillness and taking in my last memories of the Rhine. It has a slightly different feel at this time of day. After a while, I decide to end my time at the Rhine and head back for a shower.

I am nearly at the door of the hotel and when I glance at a group of people eating. I stare at this young lad's face before me and he stares back. It feels very strange, like time is standing still. I take a few steps forward for the hotel door, and pause. My brain is trying to process what I have just seen, confused.

I recognise that face, but I have never seen him before. I am in Germany and I don't know anyone. Everything goes into slow motion. I turn back and take in the wider picture. Three people are sitting at the table and one of them is Ciara. Plain as day, Ciara is eating dinner outside my hotel and I can't quite compute it. I thought she was in Bad Kreuznach, an hour's drive away.

We all laugh, and Ciara looks totally unfazed and carries on eating. I insist on giving her a quick hug. Calvin explains he had just said to Ciara in that brief moment, 'I think I just saw your mum'. He must have seen a photo of me. It was the strangest situation ever. I sit down and I am introduced to Calvin and his mum, and they carry on eating. I just sit and stare. I can't believe Ciara is here in Bacharach, sitting outside my hotel eating food.

They explain that they are visiting Calvin's mum and dad in Oberwesel. Ciara thought that I had moved on already and she didn't know where I was staying exactly, we hadn't spoken much since Mainz as we are both been holidaying.

Then the lad from reception comes out and starts chatting to Calvin and it turns out he is a good friend of his and they all went to a house party last night in Bacharach while Ciara was with Calvin's friend. I mean, you just can't make this up.

Calvin re-tells the story to his friend in German, the whole thing is so funny.

It is a pleasure to meet Calvin and his mum, I am really chuffed that I got to do it. They eat up and leave in the black Porsche and I go back to my room, laughing.

Bacharach to Cologne
Monday 31st August

I am woken by church bells at 8.00 am. I have a lovely cup of tea, chill in my lovely room, and then go down for breakfast. It's as delicious as yesterday; I dive in and enjoy it all. Once I'm finished, I go back to my room for a shower, pay the bill, and leave. The envelope they give me with my receipt in is so pretty. It has a drawing of the Rhine on it, it's like a piece of art. This is a very special hotel, with so much attention to detail. I have felt very pampered.

It's sad leaving as I enjoyed it so much here. The trip to the castle, seeing Ciara last night, the peacefulness of the Rhine, this superb hotel, and this enchanting little place.

And it's nearly time to fly home.

The station is a five-minute walk from the hotel. There is no staff, and no signs, so I can't be sure which platform to get on. I can't understand the digital thing, so I check the poster timetable. It says the 10.50 train is on platform two, which doesn't feel right, but I drag my heavy bag over the bridge. Three people arrive and go to the platform opposite. If I miss my train, I have to wait an hour. It's not a bad place to have to wait, but I would rather get on the train.

Two trains whizz by and don't stop, then my one arrives and I get on. The Rhine is on my right, so I am going the right way.

I get off at Remagen, deciding to have one more stop along the Rhine before I hit the big city of Cologne. I find the way to the river, it's just a 10 minute walk. This is a nice place.

Down at the river are about five or six restaurants and lots of outdoor seating, quite different from Bacharach. I get a green tea and chill but I do get a bit fidgety. The man working here seems put out that I didn't want to eat. There are hundreds of empty seats, so I am not in the way, but it is the way he snatches away the cutlery with a huff that unsettles me. I feel bad for his business As he would probably be flat out during a normal summer.

I decide to go for a stroll along the river. It's very similar scenery to Bacharach, but it has a wide promenade and I bet it's buzzing with people on a normal day. I come to a dead-end. I can't seem to walk any further, so I decide to get on the next train. I have gone a different way back to the station, so I am not sure exactly where to go. I appear off a street and see a train in the station on the other side of a fence. I start running as it leaves in three minutes. I wobble all the way and manage to get on just as it leaves. That was close. I think there is more to explore here, but the backpack is just too heavy to drag about.

I eat my plums from Koblenz on the journey, and they are delicious. The train ride into Cologne is just as I predicted, it's like coming to Liverpool Street station. I am a little sad, the best bit of my trip is over now. I have one last room in a big city, then home.

The train arrives in Cologne and as I get nearer the glass doors by the train's exit, a darkness descends, as I notice a huge, ugly cathedral dominating the sky. It's like a dark monster waiting outside. I had no idea that it was literally outside the train station. It's the ugliest cathedral that I have ever seen and going into it was the only thing I was interested in doing in Cologne.

Before I leave the train station, I ask at the information desk about trains to the airport and the lady behind the desk kindly prints me off three pages. There are trains every 20 minutes right through the night which surprises me. Living in Cornwall is quite different. Liam used to have to miss the end of a gig to catch the last train from Truro to St Austell at 10.30 pm.

I leave the train station and find my way up steps to the cathedral, maybe it looks better inside. It just needs a good clean and it must get dirty quickly, being in the centre of the city.

There's a big square in front of it, and I decide to go ahead and find out how much the entrance fee is; maybe I will pop in later. As it turns out a severe-looking man at the door, like a security man, doesn't make eye contact with me and I walk past him into the cathedral. Entrance appears to be free so I walk around. It's not very special in my opinion, still dark and gloomy and I don't get it. Usually, I love a cathedral. I loved the Sagrada Familia in Barcelona, the little church in Mainz, the church in Český Krumlov. But this? No. I walk all the way around and out of the door. That's that done.

Cologne is huge and I go the wrong way, heading off into the shopping area, where there are hundreds of shops and smells of food and perfume. There are so many people, which is a bit of a shock after Bacharach.

About 10 people are queuing outside Louis Vuitton, and I have no idea why. It doesn't look like there's a sale on. I have never understood branded clothes. If I like it, I like it, but have never understood the logic in wearing something that says, 'I spent a lot of money on this.' I worked at Fortnum and Mason, in London, so I understand quality, and saw some seriously rich people. And lots of famous people. I have squatted on the floor with Cliff Richard, held Priscilla Presley's credit card in my hand, advised the Duchess of Kent on how to put her eye cream on, and met many, many more celebrities. But I despise the utter waste of money. Donate it to charity if you have too much. Rant over. I am just feeling a little niggly because I don't really want to be in Cologne. I wanted to be in Lille, waiting for the Eurostar. But if I had gone that way home, I wouldn't have experienced Bacharach, and that was a very special place and a special time that I wouldn't change for anything. You simply have to make the best of everything. There will be something to enjoy here.

So far, Cologne seems to be a city of contrasts. A few feet away from the people needing expensive labelled bags is an old lady begging. On several corners, as rows of shops cross at junctions, men are busking. Some of them are about my age, not youngsters. Almost professional musicians; maybe they are, it's good music.

I eventually get to the river, and it's really wide. I can't believe this is still the Rhine. It has two enormous bridges going over it. The location of the hotel is great, just by the river and not too far from the station. There must be a quicker route than the one I took. It's 3.00 pm and I am not allowed in my room until 4.00 pm, but I may as well go and ask. Luckily, I am allowed up and it's a very strange building. I think they must have bought the building next door. I climb a nice set of stairs to the first floor, head through a door, across a passageway with offices connected to it, and then up another set of stairs. I hope there's not a fire. I will never find my way out.

The man on reception has said the hot water isn't working, so to only expect tepid, not hot. He explains that not many people are staying because of the pandemic and so the water has further to go and it's not warming up. I am not sure what to say. I don't know a great deal about plumbing, but this sounds odd.

It's another bland room but the view out of my window is perfect. I could have ended up in a dive as I was trying to penny-pinch here, as I won't be sleeping much tomorrow night.

But this is a really good spot right by the river. I am very lucky, again. I can see the Rhine, the big bridge, and a little square below me with a fountain. People are milling about, and there is a huge church to my left. It's a perfect little spot and I am happy.

I was dreading Cologne a bit, back to a big city, but this spot is going to make it bearable. I am, after all, just waiting to go home now.

The room has a shower, which I probably won't be using if it's cold, and a key to a toilet across the corridor. That's quite odd. I would much prefer a toilet in my room rather than a shower, especially in the middle of the night. And a key is very strange. I have never had a key to a toilet before, not even in the hostels. And you are hardly going to walk in off the street and use it. It's up two flights of stairs. You would need a map to find it.

I dump my stuff and go straight out. I ask about a kettle on the way down and the man on the desk finds me one. It's in a see-through plastic box like it's been stored, but I am happy. It's a kettle and I can make tea in my room.

The sun is shining, and I am hungry. I found a nice-looking vegan place on the internet. One advantage of being in a city is there's a huge array of food on offer.

Google Maps takes me the eight minutes to the eating place, it has lots of tables outside and it's busy, that's always a good sign. And OMG, there is so much to choose from. It's about 10 feet of buffet with hot and cold offerings: mushrooms, grilled sweetcorn, coleslaw, roasted cauliflower, tofu dishes. It all looks amazing. It's €9.90 for a plate and you walk along the counter to fill it up, easy. The plates have dents in them so you can put hot food on one side, and cold on the other. I get a watermelon fizzy drink to go with it before going outside to sit out in the sunshine.

But, out here, there are wasps everywhere, attracted to bits of food left on the tables and two are already in my bottle of fizzy drink, drowning. I try to ignore them but it's too much and two are in my bottle of fizzy drink, drowning.

I take my tray back indoors, drowning wasps included. The food is delicious though and, whilst eating I manage it, I manage to scoop the wasps out, partly for them, but also because I don't want to accidentally drink them. They seem to survive and dry off while I am eating my food. Then they fly away.

So, what to do in Cologne? There are lots of museums, but that's not my thing. I could get on some transport and go outside of Cologne, but I don't have the energy or enthusiasm for that, or anywhere in mind to go.

So, I do what I do best. After finishing my meal, I go for a walk, heading back to the riverside near my hotel, passing over the bridge to the right. On the other side, directly opposite the hotel, are some huge, concrete steps, People are sitting, watching the world go by, taking a lunch break or meeting people.

I walk on to the other bridge and the rails are completely covered in love locks. I mean, totally covered, with not a single space to put another one, and they all glint in the sun. It's quite a sight and a whole lot of love. I am surprised the bridge has not sunk with the weight. There is a train track on the bridge but no cars.

I go back to the vegan place for a cup of tea and cake. It will be a nice treat after my walk. Unfortunately, the tea is awful. I watch the girl put the water in the glass cup, then top it up with milk. Then she puts in the tea bag. Why do people in Europe not understand how to make tea?

I pick a gorgeous peanut butter chocolate cake and go outside, hoping the tea brews a bit by the time I sit down. It doesn't. It is so pale, you wouldn't believe there was a tea bag in it. I take a sip, and it's almost cold from swimming in half-cold milk.

I can't drink it, and I was so looking forward to tea and cake. Proper tea with plant milk and a delicious cake. They have no idea how important this tea and cake are. So, I go back in. I am not good at confrontation and have been on the receiving end of stroppy and rude customers, so I am happy to pay for another. I just want a hot cup of tea to go with my gorgeous-looking piece of cake.

The girl follows my instructions, the tea bag in first, fills it to the top with water and I ask to have the milk in a separate container so that I can add it myself. She doesn't charge me, and I hope I was polite. I go back out and enjoy my tea and cake, which is delicious. The cake is moist and chocolatey with a peanut butter topping.

Then I go back to the hotel and try to book a COVID-19 test on the NHS. It is very frustrating filling out the online forms over and over for an hour, as the NHS says it can't identify me. How ridiculous is that?

I try a different tactic. I try to book a drive-through test, not a delivered one. Maybe it's a different form. It says there are no places for Wednesday, to look again after 8.00 pm. I look at 8.10 pm, 8.20 pm and half past. I try, but there are no slots to book. It wears me out, frustrates me, and feels like a complete waste of my time.

So, I try to book the one at Heathrow Airport that costs £175 by sending an email, then put my phone down and chill. I sit at the window on my chair and look down at the empty ones outside the restaurants. This pandemic has caused a lot of damage, not only from a health perspective but also for so many businesses all over the world.

My brain is in Returning Home Mode. I don't feel like I am on holiday now. There's not much to do in Cologne that interests me. I can't help wondering what the next week will bring. What if I get a test and I am positive? Where will I go for two weeks? I can't afford a hotel in Cornwall for two weeks. I can't go home. I will look for a caravan or something or put up a tent somewhere.

Luckily, I am reading a good book and get stuck in it. If I stay up late, I can have a lie-in, and the night at the airport will be easier.

Cologne
Tuesday 1st September

I was awoken at eight by my noisy neighbours, who have kids that they don't appear to be supervising. They keep running in and out of the room, letting the door slam behind them. I swear it feels like I am lying in the middle of a playground with children jumping over me. They are squealing and screaming and possibly bouncing on the beds, and it's *so* loud. They eventually go out and I fall asleep again till 11.00 am, when I am woken by the housekeeping lady and her hoover. So I make a cup of tea with my kettle and get up.

I eat the last of my plums and the last piece of cake from the vegan café yesterday; it was too big to finish there. Today, I feel like doing something touristy while I am here and think about visiting the very tall tower I can see out of my window. I have no desire to return to Cologne. It's not been my kind of place, so I might as well do something interesting. The weather looks OK, and I need to enjoy my last day.

It is bright enough to put my sunglasses on, which put a smile on my face. As I walk right along the river, I notice that I am in the bit of Cologne with the pretty houses, the bit I was searching for yesterday. I was too busy looking at the river then. I am actually in a really good spot and I'm so grateful.

I go over the bridge and try to find the entrance to the round tower, which is not that easy. I am in a busy office-y part of town. I thought the tower was touristy but I can't find a way to the entrance. There are glass buildings everywhere, and not many signposts.

When I finally find out how to get there, I learn that it's shut today. It's only open on weekends at the moment. Oh well, I saved €5.00, and it was only a time filler. I will put the money towards dinner.

To sort my anxiety out, I time a practice-run of my journey from the hotel to the train station that I'll have to do when it's time to leave, having decided to get to bed early and leave the hotel at 3.00 am. I will be walking around with my backpack on in the dark, which I am a bit anxious about. Once I've done it, I realise the journey only takes about 12 minutes, but I admit that I did get a little lost. I think I have it mapped out in my head now and, even with my backpack on, I don't think it will take any longer than 10 minutes.

With that out of the way, now I choose to just wander around the shopping area, which goes on forever. It's more a walk for the exercise. I am sure I count four H&M's. It's so big they have to repeat the shops. I hate shopping, so it doesn't fill me with joy. Quite the opposite, in fact. Horror, at how materialistic the world is. I live in Cornwall, which is a different kind of place. I grew up in Essex and lived in Ipswich for six years, so it's not like I haven't seen a bit of the country.

Cornwall is a lot different from everywhere else that I have been to. You sort of slip into its mentality. Everything is dreckly, which can be frustrating but also amazing. Shopping is not a high priority for the people of Cornwall. At least, not from what I have experienced, and the lack of shops backs that up.

The Cologne shopping area is packed with busy people and I keep my mask on even though I am outside, as people just walk in front of you or clip your elbow as they go by.

I go into a shop and buy a couple of shopping bags with 'Koln' spelt out, the German spelling for Cologne. The bags have a photo of the big bridge with the lock. I haven't bought gifts as don't want to carry them about. Next, I pop into an Aldi and get a couple of bananas, bread rolls for snacks at the airport, a box of grapes and a bottle of wine that costs €1.29. I wonder how delicious that will be. I am hoping it will help me sleep for a few hours. I also get some cheese triangles in different flavours for Phil and Maria.

There are trains every 15 minutes, according to my printout from the lady at the train station. Plus, I heard the trains in the night going over the bridge, jangling all the locks.

I drop my bags off at the hotel and go back to the vegan buffet for my meal of the day. It's as delicious as yesterday's, minus the wasps. I would eat here once a week if I lived here. I love a good buffet.

When I get back to the hotel, I sit on the wall I can see from my hotel window, and just look at the view, along with lots of other people. It's a nice spot, which is why it's busy, with the river in front, the tower that I didn't go up, the green behind and the colourful houses. It's OK, not amazing, but I have had amazing already. And for a city, it's about as good as you are going to get.

I watch the bikes go by. I have seen so many bikes in Europe, every place I have been to. The ones whizzing by me are often motorised and some have baskets with shopping in. Cycling is a serious mode of transport here. Right now, it's warm, with a slight breeze. Germany does feel safe and clean. This time tomorrow, I should be on a train from Paddington to Truro. It's difficult to comprehend. I need to enjoy the last little bit of my trip.

I see a man on a motorised scooter whizz by with a fox mask on his head, a good quality one, not a piece of tat. As he whizzes by, I see his basil brush tail. I decide it is time to return to my room, just a few feet away.

I make a cup of tea in my room and sit by the window for hours. I see all sorts of sights, and an amateur photography session going on by the fountain, with the pretty church in the background. Men are going through the bins, looking for glass and plastic to recycle. Quite a few walk by and they are good and swift, one even has a torch to look in the bin with. Some have nearly full carrier bags, others not so many. I think it's a great idea, gives people an extra income and supports recycling.

A man sits at a table down below and the waiter brings him a pint as he reads his book. He also chats a bit to the waiter, he must be a regular. He drinks it quite quickly then orders a half and sips it. As it starts to get dark, ladies with the roses appear and approach anyone and everyone. The pavement tables are almost empty, so they must be struggling as well to sell their flowers.

I must look funny sitting up here, in the window, but no one seems to be looking up at me. I sit and drink the wine. It's not bad at all for €1.29.

I get my bags all packed for the last time, my shoes ready, and my money belt ready. All I have to do is get dressed and walk out of here. I'm not having a cold shower. I paid the bill the last time I came through, even though there is a 24-hour desk. It's one less thing to do.

And I go to sleep.

Cologne to Cornwall
Wednesday 2nd September

The wine worked, and I fell asleep quickly but it could have been tiredness as well. I wake up at 2.30 am, then doze until 3.30 am, before I get up and leave.

It's dark, and eerily quiet out on the streets. The river looks nice, lit by the streetlamps and I can see trains on the bridge.

I feel confident. I know the way and the streets are lit, which is better than I was expecting. One man on a bike goes by and there is a section that's much darker than I expected, but I walk confidently and as quickly as I can with my backpack on. Then in front of the cathedral on the big square, a handful of boys are skateboarding, which is a bit random. They are polite and move out of my way.

The station is quite busy, especially at 4.00 am. I find my platform and the train arrives at exactly 4.21 am. There are a few people on the platforms, but only one man in my carriage. He's up at the other end and gets off at the next stop. I am alone in a brightly lit train carriage on a train in Germany. It's 4.30 am by now and it's pitch black.

Another man gets on at the next stop, mutters hello, and goes and sits down. I don't feel in any danger at all. The timetable says I should be there at 4.35 am. It's a fast, efficient journey.

The train pulls into a station. I try to look for the name, but it's very dark and I can't see a sign. I get myself ready to get off in case it is my stop. But I see it's not and sit back down with my bag still on my back. It won't be long now. I perch on the edge of the seat.

And here we are at Koln Airport. The platform is dark but lit well. I realise that I have to make a decision. I thought I would just get off, but no; I have to choose: T1, 2, or 3. Oh.

I get my phone out and see who I am flying with. I am so not bothered about this flight that I don't even know who is flying me home.

Eurowings, I get off. The platform is now completely empty. The few people that were here knew where they were going and have gone. I find a glass lift and get in, like Willy Wonka, and arrive at a platform with signs to follow. I work out what to do and arrive at Departures.

Next, I sit down and sort out my bags. I have an extra one with snacks, so I sort myself out and go to the check-in desk. But the lady says that I haven't booked in. Drat. I forgot you are supposed to do this online now. How on Earth am I going to figure that out? She says for €5.00 she can do it, so I breathe out.

I leave my backpack on the conveyor belt with the lady and it's the strangest feeling ever. It's been with me for a month.

Then it's time to go through security. Among all the big moving baskets, I stand with a bottle of water in my hand and a punnet of grapes in the other. I ask if there is anywhere to empty my water like at Bristol, where there is a sink, but he says no, to throw it away. But this is my little pink Sistema bottle that I have carried the whole trip and I am not throwing it away.

So, I have to reverse and go to the toilets and empty it. When I return, my boarding card won't let me back in. I explain that I went to empty my water, and the lady says, 'I know,' with raised eyebrows. I look around and two security men on the other end are staring at me. They have all been watching my every movement, from eating grapes out of the carton, rustling in my bags, going in and out of security, wandering around aimlessly and looking like I have lost the plot. I must stick out like a sore thumb.

The security man finds my toffee hammer, to break a window on the train and doesn't look amused. He confiscates it. Ever since I heard a man on TV talking of a train crash where his daughter died on the train because the windows wouldn't open, I have always carried a toffee hammer. To break a window on a train, should it crash and I can't get out. But the security guard is not interested in my tale and takes it off me. Most trains do now have hammers for emergency use. After that, they let me through security and I am free to go.

I go and find B51 and sit down and make myself a banana roll. I was going to treat myself to a cup of tea, but not at €4.50, they can keep it. It will probably be horrible, anyway.

I check my emails. I haven't had confirmation exactly about my test, just that if I come before 12.00 pm, it will be OK. And I have no idea which terminal I am landing in, how to get to Terminal 5, or where it is.

The plane is about a quarter full so I have no one next to me, behind me or in front, which is reassuring from a COVID-19 point of view. I am not excited about returning home like you usually would be, as I am not going home. I want to hug Phil, sleep in my own bed, have a cup of tea out of my favourite cup. So, this is a halfway point between holiday and home.

The plane journey is a non-event, which is good and we land at Heathrow, back to English signs and English accents.

I stand to one side and put the postcode in my phone for the testing place and it says it's a 50-minute walk away. I can't believe it. I am on a tight timescale. I need to get the test done and get across London to reach Paddington for the long five or six-hour journey back to Cornwall.

I am so annoyed and tired. Where on Earth do I need to go? I thought I had to go to Terminal 5. Google recommends a bus, so I try to think straight. What bus? From where? I take a deep breath. Let's just get this done. The bus arrives on time a couple of minutes after I find the bus stop, so maybe it will be OK? I show the bus driver my phone and the location that I need to be at and he said he will tell me when we are there.

We drive around the big roundabouts that leave the airport and go into a residential area. I have absolutely no idea where I am. Then he stops and calls out to me. It's my stop.

I get off. I am on the very wide, dual carriageway, and not really near anything at all. I switch Google Maps on and it says I am still a 50-minute walk away.

I could cry. I don't know what to do. Why did he drop me here? Why would he do that? I need a taxi, but I don't know any numbers, or where I am. I ring the test centre to say I am on my way and trying to get there. While I think about it, and what I should do, I start to walk the way Google says. I see taxi go by, but it's on the other side of the road, so I keep walking. My bag gets heavier and heavier. I don't seem to have gone very far at all along this huge, long road. I see another taxi, this time on my side of the road, but there's a big grass verge, so it's not possible to flag him down.

I just have to keep walking. The numbers slowly go down and I am almost out of energy. I could just stop and cry my eyes out. I am so stupid sometimes. Why didn't I just get a cab from the airport, or put Google Maps on when I was on the bus?

I take a deep breath and walk a little faster, hoisting the bag up on my back so that it hurts less.

I overtake a lady walking her dog. I look like I am in a TA session. No taxis are coming to my rescue. I have to just get on with this. After 27 minutes, I am almost halfway, but it's horrible to think I have to do the same again. I put my shoulder back, keep walking, and think of nice things. Get it done.

I do get it done and arrive, sweaty and anxious and in pain. That was horrible and so easily avoidable.

But I am here. I am not booked in, of course not. It's not going to be that easy. I manage to persuade them that they said in the email to come this morning. I must look awful, and they go away and bring me back a clipboard and a form. I think it's going ahead and I pay the £175.00 bill. I have to go to the top floor of what looks like an old house, with steep old-fashioned steps. The lady is lovely and insists I leave my bag. Reluctantly, I leave my rucksack on the middle landing, but take my smaller one up to the top floor.

The test is not pleasant, but it is done. She seals it in the envelope and it's all over. I should know in 48 hours. I can return to the airport now and get a train to Paddington.

The journey across London goes OK but I am starving. There's a train to Cornwall in 10 minutes or an hour. I need something to eat so i think I will catch the later one. There's no food being served on the trains right now because of the virus. In the meantime, I go over to the ticket office to book my reservation; it's included in my Interrail ticket, but I need to reserve it. But the lady at the ticket office tells me that I can't get the train leaving in an hour, because it's full, so I have to go right now or in three hours. Unfortunately, I have to run for it, without anything to eat. At least there is a sense of relief that I am on my way to Cornwall, and the test is done.

My train should get in at about 4.00 pm . Shortly after, Phil has to pick Maria up from Flicka, our local donkey sanctuary, at 4.45 pm. What shall I do, just go get in my car and wave at him from afar, or wait till he has gone, as I will want to hug him and I can't? He can't even pick me up from the train station, as we can't be in the same car. But I need to get back to the house for my car to drive to the hotel in Newquay.

We text on the train and decide that a socially distanced, quick cup of tea on our veranda is a good idea. The veranda is a posh word for two chairs outside the front door, but it makes me smile. We sat on the veranda a lot over the summer.

The train is full of noise and rubbish conversations. I feel a sensory overload. I can understand all six conversations all over the carriage. I want to mute it all out. Most of it is garbage, a group of teenagers talking utter waffle to each other, swearing a lot. It's all too much and I don't want to listen to it. The conversations in Europe might have been rubbish too, but I couldn't understand them. We all talk too much. I have hardly said anything in a month.

Not long after arriving in Cornwall, we go through St Austell, my home for 19 years, and I know that I am now 20 minutes from Truro. I put my bag on, and get my ticket ready. I want to be out of here and in the taxi straight away as time is short.

I am right at the front as we all pile into the station, except that it won't open the barrier. The man in charge is quite horrible and points out my Interrail ticket is not an actual train ticket. I thought it would work. It's what the lady gave me in London and I have shown my Interrail ticket to the inspector on the train, so I didn't think I would have to do it all again.

I have to take my big bag off and get in everyone's way while I reach for my money belt and get out my Interrail ticket. By the time I get outside, the taxis have all gone. I only have about half an hour till Phil has to pick Maria up and I am really annoyed. I have to wait 15 long minutes for a taxi and eventually get home £13 poorer.

As soon as I get there, I am so happy to see Phil and we stay two metres-plus apart, outdoors, or all this has been for nothing, and I have a much-needed tea from my own cup, just the way I like it. Phil has even bought a cake from the Spar shop, which I devour, as I am starving. We chat away easily, as always. It's lovely to be with him again. He has to soon get Maria, so we part company.

I get in my car, drive to Newquay, and check into the hotel. When I got here, I couldn't park the car in the hotel carpark so had to reverse out, embarrassingly as someone was trying to get in. Instead, I parked up on the headland. It is so strange to have been all over Europe and now spend two days in a Cornish hotel, a place that I am very familiar with. I have spent a lot of time at Fistral this summer, as Ciara lives here, but she is still in Germany. I did think of staying at hers, but it's shared accommodation and it would have been awkward, and probably not allowed, and I think having a single room and keeping myself to myself is the best thing to do.

This place, The Carnmarth Hotel, is lovely. I have walked past it lots of times but never thought to stop and go into the restaurant. On my birthday in March, we stayed over at Pentire for the night and I can see it now over the other side of Fistral beach.

Upstairs, I am in the eaves of the hotel in a single room, on the top floor, with a Velux window that I can't see out of because the rain is so bad. Welcome to Cornwall.

I chill on the bed and sort out my photos. I did order some to be sent home during my trip, and when I got back earlier, Phil gave them to me, so now I have the first lot. It's lovely to have the photos in my hand and I spend the evening looking through them. I also message Tami, and she says she will come over to visit tomorrow for a socially distanced catch-up on the beach, which is really kind of her and something to look forward to. I go down to the bar and get a cider and chill in my room, sorting out my photos on the computer and which ones to order. It's quite overwhelming looking at it all, spanning so many places from the French mountains to hot and sweaty Venice and the Panoramic-Express. It's all been a huge adventure.

It's a huge cliché to say that life begins outside your comfort zone, but it is very true. I was uncomfortable dangling in the ski lift with Liam in Morzine, but what an experience, and the views were phenomenal. Getting my selfie stick out was nerve-racking. I know a lot of people are totally comfortable with that, but I wasn't. I gained a lot of confidence from persevering. And looking at myself so often, something that I usually avoid, was good for me. I feel more comfortable in my own skin. I am 55 years old and I look it and I am OK with that. The trip in the tin boat in the caves was scary but I overcame my fears and felt so proud of myself.

So, here I am in Newquay in a hotel instead of home, but it's not bad either. How can I possibly complain? There aren't any words to describe what an amazing month I have had.

Cornwall

Thursday 3rd September

The hotel's breakfast is amazing, with a lovely view out of the window across Fistral beach. Well, it would be if it wasn't Cornish mizzle, but I can just see the beach, through the mist. I have a full vegan fry-up, it's amazing, and a decent cup of tea with soya milk. Europe was amazing, but the tea in England is the best.

I go back to my room; I have a whole day to entertain myself. Tami will be over later, but for now, I will do an important job. I take everything out of my rucksack and list it all. What was useful and what was not. I did the same packing it, so I will have a comprehensive list, for anyone who is interested, of what worked and what didn't.

Then, I repack it properly, have a shower, and chill on my bed.

Seeing all the photos last night was almost unbelievable. Have I really whizzed around Europe on my own with a big backpack? The photos prove that I did, but there are so many of them, I stayed in so many places; it feels like I have had 15 holidays.

As I have lots of free time and all my travel journals with me, I total up all my adventures. I went on 45 trains, 14 buses. I went to 10 countries and slept in 16 beds. That's what you call an adventure.

Am I happy with all my choices? Of course I am, it was a huge success.

Would I change anything? Maybe. I would have liked an extra day at Lake Bled to explore more, maybe an extra day in Venice. Skipped Zagreb altogether. Picked a better room in Gyenesdiás, or not stayed there at all. I probably should have eaten better, had a few more hot meals, and fewer crisps.

But the experiences that I had were all important and staying anywhere longer meant missing out on another location. And I will remember that strange lake in Gyenesdiás forever.

The whole trip was a mixed bag, and I am glad that it was.

The only thing I would honestly change is spending more time on the Panoramic-Express. I should have put more research into where to get off and maybe stopped at two or three places. It was over way too quickly. But I will hopefully return one day.

I have returned safely without losing my passport, or money, or damaging myself, so I am very happy about that. Whether that was because of the procedures that I put in place, my money belt, locks on bags, or just sheer luck, we will never know.

I have enjoyed writing my journal, thinking about the life that I have lived, the good decisions that I have made, and coming to terms with the bad decisions. I think I have done OK. I definitely did the best with the hand that I was dealt. There are so many positives. I have fantastic kids, all four of them, and some really good friends that maybe I should spend more time with.

I probably owe my independent streak to my mum. She liked to travel in her spare time. It was mainly on bus trips because her circumstances were different from mine and we are different people. But I do remember her going on mystery bus trips when she didn't know where she was going. Often with her Salvation

Army friends in Harlow. And even those adventures when we were children gave us a sense of exploring.

No one's life is perfect. Mine hasn't been, for sure. Some of my memories are so painful that I get angry I had to endure them. Other people may not have been through what I have, but maybe they have been through something else that was even worse. It wasn't fair what happened to me and it's not fair what happens to other people. But it's behind me and it has made me who I am. A strong, independent person who appreciates the little things in life and tries to find joy in every day.

We can only do the best that we can with a situation that we find ourselves in. Maybe we have made wrong choices somewhere along the way, but if they felt right at the time, then they were the right ones. I survived, and now I feel like a bird freed from its cage. My children are all independent. I don't have any money worries, at last. I have a wonderful man in my life who allowed me the freedom to do this trip because he respects and loves me and doesn't want to own me.

So, if your life has been a challenge or a struggle for whatever reason, try to accept it. Move forwards, try to come to terms with the baggage, and park it somewhere. If you feel the need to go travelling, then go. If you want to go on an adventure, go on one. It really is as easy as buying a ticket and going.

I put the photos down and check my emails, seeing I have one from the testing centre.

Oh my. I was hoping it would come in early, but it's not lunchtime yet.

I can't open it. This is huge. If it's positive then I have to quarantine. If it's negative, I can go home. Oh my, I am shaking.

I open the email. It's negative. I almost cry with relief.

I send it to Phil and ring him. I don't tell him anything, just ask him to open his email and see what it says. 'It's negative,' he says. 'You can come home.'

I am close to tears.

Tami was coming to visit me later, and I feel a bit bad cancelling on her. It was kind of her to want to come over and keep me company but I message her and she totally understands.

My bag is packed and I go down to reception and check out. At first, the lady thinks something is wrong, but I explain what has happened and she is happy for me. I explain that I haven't done anything legally wrong by staying here. I have not been to any country in the last 14 days that I wasn't legally allowed to go to, or need to quarantine after. I could have gone home, but morally this was the right thing to do.

She says if she can let the room for tonight, she will refund me, which is very kind.

I walk out of the hotel with my rucksack and drive myself home.

More info, some tips and tricks

What I took with me and whether it was useful

- Lace-up Skechers. Worn on every travel day, so comfy.

- Long cotton trousers with pockets, bra, knickers, black short-sleeved top (good, went with everything), trainer socks (needed another two pairs), black zip-up cardigan.

- My money belt with Interrail ticket, passport, money.

- Drawstring bag with toothbrush, toothpaste, two throwaway razors, deodorant, collapsible brush with mirror, wash scrunchie in a plastic bag, 30 ml shampoo, tiny conditioner, three small shower gels that I picked up in hotels, (but I didn't need them all as I got more), eyeliner pencil, small soap, (which wasn't needed as hotels have soap), flannel which I threw away

- Packing cube containing small Impulse spray, Tyrozets, small scissors, lip balm, small booklet of nail files (but only needed two small ones), Imodium (which, thankfully, I didn't need but would take again), six earbuds, tweezers, 24 paracetamol tablets (which was too many), Vitamin B spray, toothpicks, hair clips, multivitamin tablets (just the right amount), small face cream, earplugs (which I didn't use), plasters, small sun cream, small after-sun, earphones, and plasters (took too many).

- Packing cube with tea bags (which I left in Lake Bled), face mask, loose green tea, two chargers for phone (left one in a hotel so glad to have had two), two converter plugs, zip-lock bags, belt, Poundland plastic coat, Giffgaff spare sim card, two pegs, spare phone, two locks for the bags and one for the lockers in hostels, passport, Interrail ticket, bank card, Monzo card, Post Office card, English money and a random bag of currencies from my children's trips.

- Packing cube with one bra (would have liked one more as it was hot and needed washing more), knitted socks, three knickers, thin dressing gown, thin hand towel, belt.

- Four notebooks.

- Two small Sistema water bottles.

- Walking sandals. A must: I used them when not on a travel day.

- Flip-flops. Great for hostels and chilling.

- Swimming costume. Didn't use.

- Thin shawl. Didn't use.

- ¾ length cotton trousers. Didn't wear much, I needed pockets.

- Red and black cotton, sleeveless top. Very useful.

- Vest top. Didn't wear in case I got sunburnt.

- Black, sleeveless top. Good.

- Purple, thin top. Good.

- Long cotton trousers with pockets. Could have done with a second pair, wore on every travel day.

- Thin dress for near a pool. Didn't wear, there just wasn't an occasion.

- Black and white skirt. Very useful, wore a lot.

- Denim shorts. Very good.

- White, thin cardigan. Did wear but didn't like, was in my charity pile.

- Sewing kit. Didn't use it but might have done.

- Two sun hats. Only needed one, but had I lost one, I would have needed it.

- Small binoculars in a waterproof bag. Not needed.

- Two plastic boxes for food. Only needed one.

- Three pens. Good.

- Selfie stick. Lots of fun.

- Second pair of glasses. Didn't use but would take a spare again.
- Three pairs of prescription sunglasses. Left one with Liam.
- Power-pack. Yes.
- Kindle. Brilliant.
- Two books. Left with Liam.
- Black and white shorts. Very uncomfortable, threw away.
- Three thin, white short-sleeved tops. Threw away gradually as the trip went on. They were in my charity pile, so I knew I would throw them away.

Things I bought on the trip

- Navy blue top which I wore.
- Blue dress I bought in Ljubljana and wore a lot.
- A second dress. Didn't wear.
- Few gifts in Cologne.

What I would add next trip

- Two more white, short-sleeved tops.

- Thin, black top for black and white skirt.
- Second pair of comfy shorts.
- Another useful dress.
- One more bra.
- Second pair of long cotton trousers with pockets.

Tips for the trip

- Get as much information as you can at the train station before you leave, so you are prepared for your onward journey.
- Screenshot maps of directions to your hotels in case there is no Wi-Fi, or data doesn't work.
- Visiting big cities for two or three hours is tough with a heavy bag.
- Eat when you can, when you see something suitable.
- Think about the currency of your next destination.
- Use up coins as they weigh heavy.
- Write down the name of your train destination and time on a piece of paper to help with communication. I went to many places that I couldn't begin to pronounce.
- Don't go out at night.

- Always lock your bag in hotels and hostels.

What I Spent
Cost of the trip: £2,570.50

- Two-month Interrail Pass – £385

- Osprey women's Fairview 70 travel pack. Capacity 57L plus 13L removable day pack. An amazing bag that I would highly recommend – £115

- Selfie stick, padlock, adapter – £24

- Travel, such as bus tickets instead of train, reservations – £130.15

- Extras, like cable cars, entrances to places – £127

- Food and drink – £439.30

- Accommodation, mix of hotels and hostels – £984.53

- COVID-19 expenses, plane home, COVID-19 test and hotel – £365

Thank you, reader

If you have enjoyed *I Hope There's a Kettle in My Room,* do check out the other titles by Paula Rooney:

Odd Poles and Baggy Trousers on the Camino de Santiago
Tinsel and Tapas: Solo in Andalucia, Searching for Christmas

And please spare a couple of minutes to leave a review, as it helps other potential readers to know a bit more about the book and makes the author very happy.

Please also follow Paula on social media to find out when her next book is being released and where she is travelling next.

Follow @PaulaRooneyAuthor on Facebook, Instagram and TikTok.

Sign up to her newsletter at www.paularooneyauthor.co.uk.

Paula is also available for book talks and book festivals. If you choose any of her books for a book club, then feel free to reach out for Questions and Answers.

Contact her via email: paularooneyauthor@gmail.com

Printed in Dunstable, United Kingdom